RISE UP FOR YOU

Closing the Gap Between You and Your Potential

Nada Lena Nasserdeen

In beloved memory of my parents, Nabih Nasserdeen and Adele Kansao Nasserdeen.

Your love and strength will never be forgotten.

TABLE OF CONTENTS

PREFACE

Writing this book over the past few years has been a journey. Parts of its composition have taken place around the world, from Thailand to Lebanon, Norway to my home in California. What I hope to have written is a unique compilation of **my story** and the lessons I've learned about rising within, **research** on how and what defines who we are and our success, and **a workbook for you** to practice and hopefully implement some of my methods and insight into your own life—as I take you through a journey in each chapter. As you read, I encourage you to pause and reflect on your own journey, truths, and untapped potential that maybe you haven't considered before.

First, there are a few important things to know: inserted throughout the book are spaces for moments of personal reflection designed for you to check in with yourself. Take these moments to really be in touch with your thoughts and carefully consider your next steps.

Secondly, you will notice highlighted selections throughout the book. These are what I like to call "golden nuggets"—little gems of wisdom and motivation that I picked up along the way, and hopefully they resonate with you too. Similarly to you reading the book, writing the book evoked recollections and sparked feelings in me. As I wrote, I hoped sharing all of my thoughts provided

the most genuine experience for you as we seek creating transformation at its deepest level.

The purpose of this book is to provide guidance and the creation of a safe space where you can be transparent with yourself and really examine your own feelings and thoughts about success, who you are, and who you want to be. I only ask that as you read, you remove all judgment, shame, and the "I should" mentality. The journey to rise up for you is not wrapped perfectly with pink bows and glitter paper. Our lives are not straight paths, but curvy roads that eventually lead us to the top of a mountain we were meant to travel... as long as we trust in what's ahead.

This book is for the leader, the working professional, the parent, and any other individual who strives to be better every day. It is written honestly from the bottom of my heart. Full transparency: I often struggled with telling my story throughout the book, but it's important to recognize that who we are as professionals is also a reflection of our personal selves—those two things are not separate. How we show up in the community, at work, and for others is all connected. So I encourage you to open your heart and mind, and allow these words to sink in.

Introduction

The greatest tragedy today is wasted human potential. Let that sink in for one second.

I'll say it again, "The greatest tragedy today is wasted human potential." Do not let this be your story.

As a past performer, former executive, college professor, and now an entrepreneur, I have seen it all. Individuals around the world, who are smart, educated, and overly capable, sabotage their success in both the professional and personal areas of their lives.

This tragedy by far is one of the worst diseases that we must cure within ourselves, within our team members, and within our community. Imagine a world where people put their best foot forward regardless of any fear they felt? What would the world look like if people led with empathy and carried themselves with the utmost confidence. Just imagine how much more productive and efficient our workplaces would be, how much more loving we would be to ourselves, and what youth and the next generation would like with such role models around them.

As I write this introduction, we are in the middle of the COVID-19 pandemic, protests and civil unrest scattered across the United States due to racial injustices our country has seen for decades. And with this unique nexus of events—a complete transformation of society and workplaces as we once knew them. The fundamentals of life that we thought meant success have come crashing down for many of us. People have gotten used to the "make a paycheck" mentality that our entire existence has become defined by it.

The pandemic has crushed the job market and destroyed financial stability for many, forcing families into their homes for months. We see that our once glorified ideas of "success" and "living the good life" may not be what we thought they were all along.

But what if that wasn't the case? What if every morning we woke up and put our best foot forward? What if we unlocked newfound pieces of our infinite greatness simply because we owe it ourselves? What if all of the challenges, hurts, and heartbreaks that we've all experienced actually contributed *positively* to our lives instead of putting shackles around our feet, preventing us from *living* forward?

Your time is now to make a difference in your life, in your workplace, and in the world. What do you need to **Rise Up For You** *and close your potential gap once and for all?*

CHAPTER 1
What Will It Take to Rise Up For You?

CHAPTER 1

I'm sitting on a thin mat on the floor of a temple on the other side of the world, in Thailand. Solemn statues encircle and look down at me, the monks' rhythmic chanting echoing through the halls. Suddenly, I begin to sob uncontrollably. Why? I ask myself —though I already know the answer. I had run off to explore Thailand because I needed to experience a new world. I needed an opportunity to escape the last two years in my head. I needed a place to get away, reflect, and understand. And I was finally arriving *somewhere*—something inside was beginning to awaken.

Let me take you back to the very beginning. I was born in Pennsylvania on August 17th, 1983, to two amazing parents: my father, Nabih Nasserdeen, who was an immigrant from a small village called Baalshmy in Lebanon, and my mother, Adele

Nasserdeen, who was born in Pennsylvania to Bahia Kansao, also of Lebanese descent.

I start by introducing my parents because everything I am and continue to be is because of them. The gratitude I feel toward my mother and father is immeasurable, and no words can truly express how blessed I feel to have been given them as parents.

Think about this. Everything we are today (as individuals) is a result of our past experiences—our traditions and backgrounds, our parents, our childhood. Few are fortunate to be born into a family with parents who love unconditionally and for that I am forever grateful.

Ever since I was a young girl, I felt unstoppable. If there was a part I wanted in the high school play, I went for it; if I wanted to be on the cheer team, I tried out; if I wanted to sing, I joined the choir. Even when I failed, I stood back up and tried again. That was the case in trying out for the cheer team—a two-try attempt until I finally made it.

Failure was never an obstacle for me as a young girl, and I always felt it was due to the love and words of affirmations I received from my parents. Every day driving to school, my mom recited little mantras to me and my brothers, and we would repeat them back with excitement and joy: "You're beautiful!" "You're going to have a great day today!" "You're going to get a good education!" These affirmations excited and motivated us to go out there and give everything we had. My mother was smart enough to know that the *manner* of your self-talk could either destroy you or make you better. She wasted no time in teaching us how to have positive conversations with ourselves. But that actually wasn't enough. Saying these words of affirmation was only one piece of the *yin-yang* of fully stepping into life.

My father had the opposite approach—I like to call it "the philosopher's way." When he noticed that I wasn't using my full potential, he would call me out in a way that as an adult, I have embraced wholeheartedly. I vividly remember bringing home a test where I'd gotten an A-. I was so proud of myself! But when I showed the test to my father, he just looked at me and said, "Where's the A+?"

I was shocked. I looked back at my dad and said, "Dad it's an *A minus*—that's pretty good!"

He put the paper down and said the words that changed my life forever: "Nada, are you capable of getting the A+?"

"Of course," I replied.

"Do you believe you can get the A+?"

"Yes."

"So why *didn't* you get the A+?"

I paused in thought.

Then he said, **"If you know you have what it takes, why wouldn't you use your full potential to do it?" (Golden Nugget #1)**

Now I know what you're thinking: okay, this is a little harsh—for goodness sake, it was an *A-*. But that's irrelevant. My father's point was: if you have everything you need to succeed and give it your all, why *wouldn't* you do it?

He asked me questions that made me reflect on the decisions I made—on the outcomes that resulted because of them. Between my mother's words of affirmations and my father's "philosopher's way," the idea of going for it and using my full potential quickly became a daily, non-negotiable personal mantra.

PRACTICE: What is your daily mantra and how does it serve you?

_____

_____

By the time I was 21 years old, I was touring the world as a performer with an incredible non-profit organization which promotes the empowerment of people through the universal language of music. For years, I traveled across the globe with a cast of 40 performers, making my mark on stage as a lead singer while also providing hope and happiness to the audiences I performed for.

My journey as a performer was personally invaluable, but more importantly, the experience opened my eyes to the struggles of different people on different levels.

I admit that when I was younger, I was fairly closed-minded about what it meant "to struggle." Having parents from a third-world country, my idea of "pain and suffering" were things like war, poverty, and social injustice. Traveling with a multicultural cast of 40 for three months at a time tested my nerves and sense of the world just as I was entering into adulthood. It sort of boiled down to this: I had almost no compassion or empathy for those around me who complained about their lives. I perceived in some of my fellow cast members that they just lived with constant baggage—all this *weight*, always having something to complain about. Now, whether or not feeling like this was fair, it was foreign to me and turned me off from befriending them.

Looking back now, all I can say is we all have moments in our lives when we are not our best selves, and this was one of them for me. But my mentors in the organization, Bill and Robyn Brawley, really opened my mind to understanding true compassion and love for all. We had many conversations—sometimes arguments—about seeing people compassionately and without judgment. It has definitely been a process, and sometimes I still have to remind myself that everyone has a different story, about which we know nothing. And most importantly, we all handle our experiences differently!

On tour, the main thing that really got under my skin was the lack of confidence and self-worth I saw in so many of my fellow cast members. When I was younger, I couldn't understand the "I'm not good enough" mindset. I always had major solos in the show; I always stood center stage, which is the coveted spot for a performer. With all that said, I was *never* the best singer on tour. There were always two to three singers who naturally had a better sound and technique than I did. They could sing me out of the water! Sometimes I would be on a tour with cast members who had a full octave range more than I did—for all you singers out there, that's over a three-octave range. Yet every tour—all 12 tours to be exact—I was the lead female vocalist.

My dear friend on tour told me one day, "You're so good. I wish I had what you had. I wish I could have those solos!"

I looked at her and without hesitation said, "You're a way better singer than I am."

Everything you need is already inside you. The only difference between you and me is I actually believe that I'm good enough to stand here." (GN #2)

I don't share this anecdote to brag about how great I am. Rather, I share it to highlight how many of us are *holding back* our true selves and gifts from the world—not anybody else preventing us. How many of us are showing up in a room full of people with our shoulders hunched over, staring at the floor? Being on 12 tours, performing alongside these other talented young men and women revealed to me how many capable, beautiful people are sabotaging their success and lives because of their self-deprecating thoughts and habits.

Touring in Ireland in 2005 at the age of 22, I realized that my true calling was not, in fact, to be a performer, but to somehow empower others to believe in themselves, so they could manifest the success they only dreamed about. I didn't know how to do it or what it looked like, I just knew my true calling was slowly starting to reveal itself from the stage lights of our tour.

After spending years on the road and away from my parents and siblings, I could feel in my heart that it was time to come home and settle in one place. In January 2012, I decided to hang up my microphone, stow my beat-up tour luggage, and dive into my deep passion of education and leadership. Within a year, I stepped into a new world—the corporate world. Then at 27 years old, I was asked to become the Executive Director for an education corporation who had a number of on-site schools throughout California. Working hand-in-hand with the CEO of the company, I knew my next chapter was bound to be significant as I went from the stage to the board room within a year. I was excited, hungry for growth, and ready to make an educational impact on thousands of students and faculty members.

When I started my new position, I was shocked to see that it wasn't, in fact, the students who needed the most mentorship, but the professionals who were working alongside me. Increasingly, I saw employees sabotaging their professional careers, holding their tongue even though they had something to say, and worse, putting down and talking bad about the other team members they worked with. This shocked me as I had the naive perception that this only took place in the entertainment world—a world where often there is a lot of judgment about how you look and whether or not you fit "the mold."

How wrong I was! In this new world full of educated professionals—many of them older than me—they displayed the same lack of confidence, self-doubt, and feelings of meaning as the performers I knew on tour. Not only was this clearly affecting their work performance, it was also dampening their happiness and ability to truly make an impact on their students. Accomplished professionals of all ages with Master's degrees and PhDs were struggling to speak their truths and live their best and most fulfilled lives.

The most heartbreaking part was that, at one point, many of these incredible people wholeheartedly loved what they did, but somewhere along the line, something or someone brought them down and affected how they showed up in the world—how they parented, how they mentored their students, how they developed relationships with others, how they formulated conceptions of themselves.

These colleagues did not lack ability. Rather, their problem was a lack of confidence to step forward and try—and the perfectionist mindset that many of us suffer from.

Perfectionism equals prevention and therefore is not wanted! We must allow ourselves the space to grow and learn through the journey. (GN # 3)

In the spirit of full transparency, I admit that it took some time for me to develop a real sense of compassion toward others. My initial reaction was "What's the problem? If you want something, go get it! If you have something to say, just flipping say it already! If you're not happy, change your circumstance! It's that easy, right? 1-2-3 and you can make a shift!"

WRONG! I was way off base and pretty judgmental now that I think about it and write it into words. It's not 1-2-3, and it's not that easy! This epiphany did not come easy for me.

There's an old quote: "What goes up must come down." And that's exactly what happened!

What Goes Up Must Come Down

At 29 years old, I felt proud of myself and the accomplishments I had achieved thus far in life. I had a six-figure income in a career field I was passionate about, a home on the lake, a new luxury car, all the water toys one could imagine, and an incredible family by my side. Everything I wanted I had, and when I turned 30 years old, the last thing on my wishlist came to fruition. A beautiful, Middle Eastern man came into my life and asked me to marry him. Yes, my life plan was coming true! Work hard, travel the world, get a great education, make great money, and finally, find Prince Charming, get married, and have babies! It was all perfect!

I remember the first time I met Amar at a community picnic. His personality just seemed to shine brighter than everyone else's. His smile stretched from ear to ear with big dimples and big bold eyes. He was interested in me and asked me a ton of questions. I thought, "Wow, he's really interested in knowing who I am!" His genuine curiosity was a quality I had been yearning for at the time.

Amar was kind, had great energy, was very successful, and we connected on a cultural level, which also meant a lot to me. He had a big personality that was strong, clear, and captivating.

We continued to develop a long-distance relationship—me in America and Amar in Canada. It grew fast; we traveled every other week to see each other, and before either of us knew it, we were in love! I could barely think about anything else except him. I was distracted at work and constantly looking at my phone.

I guess this is it, he's the one, I thought. So when

Amar asked me to marry him four months later, there was no hesitation! ...well, except one.
Not only did Amar ask me to marry him, he asked me to move out of the country. It was a scary moment for me as I would have to leave my family and everything, I had built for myself. It took me some time to get comfortable with the idea, but at

the end of the day, I knew I could rebuild my professional self wherever I went.

Remember, you make the career; the career doesn't make you! (GN#4).

After many conversations with myself, I decided to take the leap for love. After all, in my heart, my deepest desire was to be a loving wife and mother. No job or amount of money could give me that. So, I began preparing. I sold most of my belongings, got rid of my car, moved out of my house, and put in my notice of resignation for the end of the year.

During our engagement, I started to recognize some of Amar's characteristics that didn't sit well with my foundational values, and it made me nervous. The energy between us had begun to feel a little tense. His glowing dimples I hardly noticed anymore, and it seemed to me that his taking an interest in who I was and what I was doing was quickly becoming more of a bother to him. My intuition was flashing red, and yet I ignored my feelings. Everything will be alright— he is probably just stressed, I thought. I can't expect perfection from him. We will grow together!

I started compromising who I was to prevent arguments. It felt like I was walking on eggshells 24/7. I could feel myself losing my identity, and nothing is worse than looking in the mirror and not being able to recognize who you are.

The worst part was that my mother was starting to see it. One night I vividly remember, she heard a conversation that Amar and I had on the phone. After I hung up, she cried and said, "Nada, please give the ring back!" I didn't listen to her and told her everything was going to be all right and not to get involved. *A mother's wisdom is always under-appreciated until one day you wake up and see that she was right.*

Side Note:
A mother's love is invaluable and irreplaceable. My mom in particular could see signs and red flags that I couldn't. Experiences from her own life, which I will not get into here, gave her the wisdom to pass on to me. Sadly, I ignored her wisdom, as many children do with their parents because I wanted to make my own decisions and live my own life!

So, the big day had finally arrived. I awoke feeling nervous, but committed. It wasn't the best feeling to wake up to doubts creeping in on my wedding day. I started preparing and getting ready in my hotel room with my cousins and my mom. Our room was overlooking the gorgeous ocean, but all I remember is that it was quiet. It was *very* quiet. Not a lot of talking, not a lot of laughing—just quiet. I started feeling stressed, going back and forth in my head about my feelings, but I was resolute —resolute enough to talk myself out of the negative thoughts I was having. I was too smart for my own good. They say the head and the heart have to work together for true alignment to occur in an individual's life. It's clear to me today, that I let my head steer the ship and convince my heart that even if there were going to be a storm, I was going to be just fine anyway.

So, I tied the knot!

The Betrayal of Oneself

There I was, in another country but optimistic about this new chapter in my life with Amar. I could feel that he was fairly stressed out and exhausted. As a new, concerned wife, I asked many times if he was okay and if there was anything I could do to support him. I felt disconnected and unsure how to navigate this new situation.

I was looking forward to our honeymoon, which was postponed for a few weeks after we got married because of work obligations. The honeymoon will be great for us both, I thought. We will get away and reconnect like the two lovebirds that we are! Thinking back now, it seems crazy to think that in less than a month of marriage we needed to reconnect again.

We finally made it to the honeymoon, and our adventures and memory-making were just about to begin. We were walking down the streets of Playa del Carmen together, holding hands, people watching, and finally enjoying our much needed holiday together. After a few hours, Amar and I decided to stop at a beautiful restaurant and enjoy our first honeymoon dinner together. I felt happy and serene as we looked over the restaurant balcony and watched the groups of people pulsing through the streets of Playa Del Carmen. Strobe lights flashed, music was bumping in the background, and vibrant energy filled the city. I looked over at Amar and could see that something was off—something in his eyes was missing. My heart started to break because I could feel that something was off.

Concerned, I asked him, "How are you feeling?"

His response was something I was not prepared for. He looked at me and said, "Marriage is harder than I thought it would be."
I was shocked! In my head, I couldn't help but think, marriage is harder than you thought? After a few weeks? Seriously?!

Don't get me wrong, I knew going into a marriage that there would be ups and downs, and I was prepared to work hard. The so-called "spark" that society constantly talks about does not last forever and is not a measurement of someone's love. However, after a few weeks and on the first day of our honeymoon, Amar's words were completely unexpected.

I immediately went into educator-mode and asked another probing question, "Okay, I understand. What's making you feel this way?"

Sometimes I wonder what would have happened if I had never asked. The next few minutes listening to what Amar had to say was one of the most painful interactions I have ever had with another human being. I sat there in stunned silence, listening to Amar blame me for his lack of happiness. A whole list of hurtful things that were obviously pent up were unleashed and I had no idea what I should do or say next.

I remember feeling like Jekyll and Hyde. One side of my heart was filled with hurt, and my mind was going a mile a minute, figuring out how to mend this. On the other side, my ego was shouting in my head, "Who the hell are you to talk to me this way? No one treats Nada this way!" As I was bombarded with his hurtful words, internally I was spiraling out of control.

The saying goes: "Sticks and stones may break my bones, but words will never hurt me." This is not true! All of the damaging words I was hearing did hurt me. I felt defeated, for the first time in my life—*defeated*.

And then it hit me. All of the people I had crossed paths with, who showed up with doubts, fears, and self-sabotaging thoughts, weren't just throwing a pity party for themselves. They didn't lack the ability to live their best lives; they were just hurt—defeated, like me. At some point in their lives, something or someone had hurt them and convinced them that they weren't good enough until they started to believe all of the hurtful words and adopted them as part of their own identity.

All painful experiences—whether they stem from childhood or adulthood trauma—affect the way we show up in the world, how we communicate with others, and how we give and receive love. Subconsciously, our past experiences can lead us down a self-sabotaging path. For some of us, it shows up in our professional careers—for others, in our romantic lives. Either way, all of us are the sum total of the situations, experiences, and interactions we have internalized throughout our lives. Whether good or bad, they affect us, and not always in the best way. After a while, everyone else's opinions about us start to become our own truth.

Before I responded, I took a few breaths. Staring at him, I could somehow see that through his harsh words, this wasn't about me. This was *his* pain. Something I learned from years of being in education and working with so many diverse people is that hurt people hurt! Many times, we are quick to blame ourselves when something doesn't work, especially in relationships.

We start to justify how shitty things could happen by pointing the finger at ourselves. "Oh, if only I had spent more time with him," or "It's my fault because I made him upset."

It's important for us to recognize that sometimes it's not about you, and no matter how perfect you are, it'll never be enough because the person you're with doesn't feel that he/she is enough. (GN#5)

As I continued looking at Amar, I finally mustered up the courage to say, "We can get through this. I'm disappointed and hurt in what I'm hearing, but we can work it out."

At that moment, I decided to leave it at that. Although I was dying on the inside, I felt it necessary to say only a few words in this tense situation. From there, it was ten long days of a honeymoon in a foreign country.

Once we returned from our honeymoon, I was confident we would be able to smooth things out with some guidance from our families. But once again, life had its own plan. Within days of returning, our marriage spiraled out of control. Within three weeks of living together, we were headed for a divorce, and I was back on an airplane to California with only two suitcases of personal belongings in tow.

PRACTICE: This story is my own, so take a minute to shake off any feelings that may have emerged as you read it. Take three deep breaths using your diaphragm; inhale for three, and exhale for three. Do this five times.

Filled with embarrassment and shame, I cried for most of the flight home. I hadn't even told my mother I was coming back home. Where was I going to work? What would I tell people when they asked where Amar was? I only have a hundred dollars in my account, how am I going to support myself? How could this happen to me—a successful, educated, professional woman who prides herself on her accomplishments? How could I be successful in everything except my own marriage? I was feeling every emotion in the book: confusion, despair, anger, I felt it all.

The flight back from Canada was the longest of my life! The stewardess must have thought I was crazy because my tears would not stop. So many thoughts were going in and out of my head that after hours of crying and mental torture, I exhausted myself and finally fell asleep. And then—as I like to call it—a miracle happened. God gave me the gift of a dream while I slept. My father met me in my dreams and said, "You worked too hard on yourself, and everything you need, you already have. *Life is too short to blame people and be miserable. Yalla (the Arabic term for let's go), rise up and live a*

happy life." (GN #6) I was only asleep for a few minutes because that dream woke me immediately.

You see my father had passed away a few years prior, so he wasn't there to see me get married. He was a strong man and the epitome of a father, husband, and friend. He came to this country from the Middle East with only $22 in his pocket, and he hustled hard to provide a life of happiness for himself and his family. Everyday he dedicated himself to disciplining my brothers and me, teaching us self-respect, and showing us that all humans are created equal: "No one is better than you; and you are no better than anyone else."

My father was a unique man who always allowed me to be myself even when it was hard for him and went against our cultural norms. As a Middle Eastern man, he did not fit the stereotypes you hear in the media. My father let me wear whatever I wanted. He came to my concerts when I was a performer—not a typical career move as most of us receive the pressure to be a doctor or lawyer—and he supported my traveling the world for months at a time. He trusted me and believed in my abilities. He didn't come to this country to build a life for his family so that we would be miserable and live a life of heartache. Most importantly my father, the most important man in my life, never knocked me down or made me feel worthless; he never diminished my value as a woman. Up until the day he died and even after his passing, he loved me and showed up as a father should for his daughter. Even after he passed, he came to me the night he died in my dreams and said, "*Baba* (Arabic term for father), don't cry, *baba*. It's okay, I knew it was going to happen. It's ok, *baba*, don't cry." After that, every dream he showed up in, I paid special attention, and this one was no different.

My short dream was a blessing in disguise. It instantly invigorated and lit a fire in me—not a feeling of envy or retaliation, but a feeling of positivity and hunger. In that moment I knew that nothing and no one was going to take back or fix what had happened. No one was going to knock on my door and give me my job back, hand me back the keys to my car and house, mend my heart, or rewrite history. After I woke up, I said to myself, "Nada, Dad's right. Nothing is going to just give you back your happiness. You have to rise up for you!"

And so it began!

The Rainbow After the Storm

When I arrived back in California, it took me about a week to process what had happened and how I was going to come to terms with it. My family was supportive but angry—actually more angry than even I was. Sometimes, people who love you hurt more for you than you can hurt for yourself.

Especially for parents, it pains them to see their children suffer; no matter how old we get, in their eyes, we are still their babies.

There I was: 31 years old and back to square one, starting from scratch and rebuilding. I suddenly found myself needing a way to make money; I had to find a place for myself. I realized I would need to forge a new dynamic for my life from the remains of my old one. What was going to motivate me? What things were going to be meaningful? I had to reinvent myself. At the same time, I knew this was a new season in my life, and I had the opportunity to craft something new and impactful—something that came from me!

A week went by as I moved out of the shocked, "everything is going to be okay" stage, and into the "I'm so freaking pissed and no person should have to go through this" stage. I realized that if an educated, professional like me could experience something so unsettling, there were probably plenty of other people who seemed "put together" on the outside who were going through similar (if not worse) things than what I was going through. I knew in my gut that I was not alone.

As women in particular, we tend to carry a lot of shame. We are scared of what others will think of us. In some cultures, it is the woman who automatically gets blamed when there are problems in the household. False accusations and assumptions crop up: "Oh, she must have done something wrong for him to react this way," or "She was probably too strong, and men don't like someone with an opinion about everything." Damaging, hurtful rumors are constantly mumbled throughout the community. If you're reading this, and you can relate to what I'm saying, know that you are not alone. All women—regardless of cultural background—fear being ridiculed and judged by others. This is why many of us do not speak up or do what is best for us when we're in fight-or-flight situations.

Now please, don't get me wrong. I am not promoting divorce or painting any gender out to be monsters. What I am saying is that too many people stay in relationships when they're clearly toxic. When things are falling apart, we hold painful feelings inside and tend to deal with issues on their own because we feel ashamed and don't want to be judged by others. There was a part of me that felt I should do the same; however, I knew deep down inside that this happened for a reason, and I wasn't going to let my shame and other people's opinions of the situation run my life. This was no longer just about me; it was about people all over the world who barely scratch the surface when it comes to living the life they deserve. Between my experiences with people in the workforce who doubted themselves and my own personal journey, I knew that whatever I was going to create *needed* to help others.

So where and how do I start? The first thing I did was to sit down and ask myself the big WHAT! *What* did I love to do? *What* did I think I was good at? *What* did other people think I was good at? That last question is pivotal because we don't often see in ourselves what others might see in us.

PRACTICE: Ask five of your closest friends, family members, or colleagues what they think you are great at. This practice should be eye-opening and provide insight on what other people see as your strengths.

Luckily, my friends, family, and I all came to a similar conclusion. All of my life I loved all things education—teaching, being taught, learning from life, growing as an individual, and helping other people grow. My closest friends and family told me that I was good at recognizing potential in others and empowering them to seek greater for themselves. They also said I was a great performer. Although my singing days were behind me, I knew performing on stage was about to take a different shape.

It was clear, my WHAT was empowering others to recognize their greatest potential and become their best. But what did that mean? Empowering others. Empowering them in what? And how was I going to do it? I was one step closer, but still not completely clear where I was going.

Once my "what" started to reveal itself, I hit the internet. It was time to get friendly with Google. I searched day and night for tips and quality education on how to become an entrepreneur and ways to build your business. I even invested thousands of dollars (and by that I mean using my credit card) on conferences and coaching in an effort to better understand social media, marketing, wording, ways of providing service... Ahhhhhhh! It was so overwhelming. It is still so overwhelming.

I hit the ground running when I came back to California. I was feeling great and on fire. I was finding my what, and I was moving forward.

Then, two weeks later? Boom, *loneliness.*

It was a harsh realization, but I finally admitted to myself that I was sad and even worse, I felt empty. I felt depleted in almost every area of life that was supposed to bring me fulfillment. Sure, I was on my way to building something exciting, but I had so many things clouding my mind that I couldn't focus.

As my new chapter in life was unfolding before me, I recognized an emptiness in me that I had never felt before—a feeling of nothingness. And I'm not referring to the spiritual awakening of nothingness that Eckhart Tolle so beautifully defines; it was a nothingness more similar to a black hole.

At that time, I had very few friends. I spent so much of my life in career mode, grinding 14 or 16-hour workdays, seeking to climb the corporate ladder. I wasn't nurturing my relationships because I was too busy making money—making a lot of money to buy things I didn't need, to impress people I didn't care about. With the exception of a handful of loyal friends, my tribe—my community had fallen apart.

After moving to Canada for love and resigning from my corporate job, my finances were in the red. With only $100 left in my bank account, I had no choice but to rely on credit. I was renting a vehicle to get around town. I had no idea what I was doing, and clearly financial management was a skill I had yet to acquire.

My former career was gone, and I was starting over. My love life was tattered, my heart broken, and my health was suffering from it all. Literally, almost all aspects, *every pillar of my life—relationships, money, career, love, and health—was in ruin.*

It was a harsh truth with which I had to come to terms. There was only one pillar that was still standing strong: *my self-worth.* Although I felt sad and lonely, I still valued and loved who I was inside.

There is a big misconception we often hear. "If you're lonely or feel sad, it's because your self-worth is low. If you feel unhappy, it's because you need to find happiness inside yourself first."

I call BS on that. Recognizing feelings and giving them a voice have nothing to do with your sense of self-love and worth; instead, it is the simple acknowledgment of your current emotional state and the reasons you feel the way you do. If your state of emotion lasts for long periods of time, or is a recurring pattern, perhaps the common denominator is yourself and how you feel inside.

My internet research continued in an effort to figure out how to rebuild all the broken pieces of my life. But this time, instead of only researching how to build a company, I eventually found myself cobbling together the idea of the six pillars. How could I build lasting connections and relationships? How should I invest my money to create financial stability? What did I need to do in order to mend my broken heart? How could I maintain a healthy lifestyle when I was stressed as hell? I was on a mission to become my best self, and I finally realized that every pillar was a contributing factor. No longer was I simply cultivating this one -dimensional professional career woman. I realized my focus needed to be on the WHOLE PERSON.

Within one month, I was moving and grooving with the development of my new company, Rise Up For You. The accompanying podcast was released, featuring experts and thought leaders from around the world who have inspired others as well as myself. The website was up and running, and a plan was in full swing to empower and educate individuals and companies to start BECOMING THEIR BEST! I was feeling great, and things were looking great! Greatness was re-emerging from within and all around.

CHAPTER 1 GOLDEN NUGGETS

If you know you have what it takes, why wouldn't you use your full potential to do it?

Everything you need is already inside of you. The only difference between you and me is I actually believe that I'm good enough to stand here.

Perfectionism equals prevention and therefore is not wanted! We must allow ourselves the space to grow and learn through the journey.

Remember, you make the career; the career doesn't make you!

It's important for us to recognize that sometimes it's not about you, and no matter how perfect you are, it'll never be enough because the person you're with doesn't feel that he/she is enough.

Life is too short to blame people and be miserable. Yalla (the Arabic term for let's go), rise up and live a happy life.

END OF CHAPTER REFLECTIVE QUESTION:

How did reading this chapter make you feel? Be honest with yourself and explain why.

_____

_____

_____

_____

_____

_____

_____

CHAPTER 2
When It Rains It Pours

CHAPTER 2

I remember it like it was yesterday. Four months after I came back from Canada and three months after I began building Rise Up For You, I was at dinner with my mother and my Aunt Camelia. It was wonderful spending time together, and the bond between my mother and me was reshaping into something different. As two women, we could finally relate to one another on a deeper level. It was no longer only about mother and daughter; we now shared a common truth and understanding as women who have endured both heartache and embarrassment.

The three of us sat together enjoying each other's company, laughing, and talking about random things when an unexpected thing happened. My mom suddenly started coughing and choking. She looked up at me with embarrassment, and then excused herself to the bathroom.

I looked at Aunt Camelia and said, "What the hell just happened?"

"It's been happening for months," she replied. "She didn't want to tell you. She's scared to go to the doctor."

My heart seized up and fear coursed through my veins. I could feel that what I just heard was not a good thing. When my mom came back, I asked her what just happened. She said this had been happening for months, and she was having trouble swallowing.

I looked at her and told her assertively, "I'm booking you an appointment with the doctor, and I will go with you to see what's going on."

She nodded sadly. I think in her heart she also knew that whatever she was going through wasn't going to be good.

As we get older and develop into adults, our parents seem to become more childlike. The circle of life takes effect, and we children begin to take care of our parents as our parents once took care of us. (GN #7)

After a few weeks, my mother and I finally set an appointment to see the doctor. As normal, tests were run, and a few weeks later, the results would be in. My mother and I sat there patiently waiting for the general practitioner to come in and tell us what was happening.

It's moments like these in life when every thought comes to your head. Thoughts of love, gratitude, fear, worst-case scenarios, and everything in between.

Finally, the doctor came in. "Hi Adele, how are you today?"

"Fine," she said.

He looked at me, looked at her, paused and said, "Adele, you have cancer."

I will never forget—she immediately replied softly, "I don't want it."

I sat there stupefied, fighting back the tears. I wanted to be strong and hopeful for her, but my heart sank. My eyes started to swell, and within seconds I could feel my whole energy shift into action mode.

"Doctor, what's the action plan, and what are our next steps? We don't have any time to waste, and my mother is going to beat this," I heard myself say.

My mom looked at me, fear in her eyes. It was at this moment I could clearly see our roles had reversed. I took on the motherly, protective role, and it was my mother who suddenly needed protection and guidance. If you have been in this situation where a loved one has been diagnosed with cancer, you know that the journey on which we were about to embark was going to forever change the course of our lives. The thought of overcoming cancer was daunting and overwhelming, no small feat.

After weeks of being tossed back and forth between various doctors, trying to get insurance approvals, and a number of subsequent tests, it was clear that my mother had stage two cancer. But it wasn't just any type of cancer—my mother had cancer of the esophagus. According to medical research and studies, the five-year survival rate of esophageal cancer diagnosed at stage two was 17%. Obviously these numbers were disheartening for us, but we also knew that we had to stay positive and continue to fight for her life.

Months went by. Finally we were admitted to see a surgeon. According to the medical team, my mother's cancer had fortunately not spread and was centralized in her throat. The good news was we could target the cancer. The bad news—this surgery was one of the most invasive procedures out there, requiring doctors to open up the middle of her chest and an additional incision in her neck. Also, due to the nature of the cancer, my mother was going on three months of not being able to eat or drink normally. She had been living off *Fiber One* drinks, which were directly tubed into her lower stomach, bypassing her throat. It had been months since my mother felt any type of sensation or taste other than saliva in her throat.

We had no time to waste. We were eager to get her surgery going, but fear that she was too skinny to make it through surgery caused the medical team to postpone her surgery date several times.

Anger welled up in me as I simply could not understand what the hell was happening and why everything was moving so slowly. I'm not a doctor, but the lack of proactivity was frustrating and evoked an energy in me that I did not like or recognize. At this point, the aggressive "you know what" came out in me—an attitude and energy I hadn't seen in myself since I was a bratty teenager.

"What are we waiting for?" I asked. "It's now April, and we still haven't planned her surgery even though you diagnosed her back in late January."

The lack of progress forced my brothers and me to switch medical teams. The new team of doctors said that my mother actually wasn't in stage two—but stage *four*—and we really had no time to waste. Additionally, the medical team told us that the chemotherapy she had been undergoing for the last four months to shrink the tumor had actually aggravated it with no positive effect—a rare circumstance among cancer patients.

One month later, the surgery was set to take place. We maintained hope as the medical team informed us that the cancer was still centralized. Our only wish then was that she would make it through the surgery, weighing just 96 pounds.

It was June 9th, 2016, 4:30 in the morning. My mother and I got to the hospital before dawn with high hopes, a palpable energy, and a night full of prayers to God that she would wake up after surgery. I remember it like it was yesterday, holding her hand before the doctors took her in. It was going to be a four to five hour surgery with a minimum 14-day hospital stay after the procedure.

The doctors came in. "We're ready for you, Adele."

I kissed my mother, wished her good luck, and said, "I'll see you in a few hours."

I was escorted into another room and she was rolled away into surgery. I sat in the waiting room, praying and crying, praying and then crying again. This ritual continued for two hours as they operated.

"Please God," I prayed, "don't take another parent away from my brothers and me again. We've already lost Dad. Give us more time, please, give us more time."

After two and a half hours of sitting in the waiting room, the doctor walked into the waiting room. My heart dropped. Holy shit, I thought to myself. Why is he out here? He still has two hours before finishing the surgery.

The doctor approached me. "Nada, we did it. We're finished. I got it all out, and I think she's going to be just fine. She's a strong woman."

I wept with joy and cried, "You scared me. It's only been two and a half hours."

"We were able to locate it and cut it right out, and I'm certain I got it all," the doctor said.

Two and a half weeks later, after happily sleeping in the hospital with my mom—the best weeks of sleep I had had in months—we were leaving the hospital. I imagined my mother, ready for this new awakened life as a cancer survivor.

I remember within the first few weeks of being home, she looked at me and said, "Nada, I want a burger from McDonald's."

I laughed. "You can have as many burgers as you want!"

Sure enough, she ate the full meal with fries and a Coke. It was amazing to see her actually enjoying food again. A simple act that so many of us—including myself—take for granted. The ability to simply swallow and to taste the flavors of food was something my mother no longer took for granted.

The Unexpected Typhoon

We had only one round of focused radiation left to ensure everything was clear and out of my mother's system—a seemingly insignificant obstacle in comparison to her last six months. But for now, it was time to celebrate! My mother and I were so happy, we decided to take a mother-daughter trip to our favorite place, Las Vegas! We enjoyed the lights, cirque shows, shopping, and of course we indulged in the penny machines, my mom's favorite. It was a joyful and memorable experience, celebrating my mother's resilience and grace that she carried throughout the whole ordeal.

When we returned, we were ready to go! My mom was dressed to the nines as always and we were off to start her final round of radiation. However, right as we were about to leave, the doctor called. I could see my mom's energy visibly shift.

After she hung up the phone, she said, "We can't go anymore."

"Why not?" I asked.

"They've found something, and said they need to see me."

Once again that burning feeling of fear had shown up and this time it was stronger than ever.

The next day we went to see the doctor to see what had changed and why they put a halt to radiation. A new doctor came in this time. Looking at us both, she said, "Adele, the cancer is in your bones and cannot be surgically removed."

"What?!" I cried instantaneously. "We were told that the cancer was contained, which is why she went through with the invasive surgery."

"We didn't detect it," the doctor said.

My mother was given three to five years to live. Okay, three to five years, I kept telling myself. That's better than a few months. We can travel the world, live our lives to the fullest, and hopefully beat this thing through the enjoyment of life.

My mother, on the other hand, was defeated. She was so proud of herself for fighting and beating her initial diagnosis and now she felt consumed by helplessness. My heart was broken and I can only imagine how she felt.

We went back home and did our best to live a normal life. With a new set of doctors and different medical treatment for the bones, we stayed optimistic. Plus, at least she could eat again, right? Wrong! After only two weeks from learning that the cancer had spread to her bones, we started seeing the same symptoms again with her swallowing. Within three weeks, she was back in the hospital without the ability to eat or swallow.

"I don't understand" I told the doctor. "We were told that the cancer was contained, which is why we went forward with the surgery. Then a month later we're told she has bone cancer—which I don't know how you didn't detect in the CAT scan she had a month ago. Now we're back in the hospital because she can't eat again even though you did the esophagus surgery. And it's only been five weeks! What the hell is happening?"

Clearly I was back to angry mode with no filter, an enormous amount of fear, and a cloud of darkness that I tried to cover up in front of my mom. We ended up staying in the hospital for four weeks while they examined my mom to understand why she couldn't eat again. I slept in the hospital room with her, showered at the *24-Hour Fitness*, continued to build Rise Up For You and did my best to live a normal life within the four walls of her in-patient room. Again, I can only imagine how my mother felt being the patient.

Finally after four weeks of hospital food, the doctor came in and said that he had to open my mother up and see why she couldn't eat. He said, "It could very well be that your feeding tube is knotted up and causing you to regurgitate your food. Let's get you into surgery tomorrow and get this taken care of so that you can go home."

Feeding tube knotted up? Easy fix, right? The doctor seemed optimistic and once again I could feel a little light shining down on us. In no time we would be back home embracing our last years together.

SURGERY #2

So the day was here again, but this time under much different circumstances. Surgery in, fix the tube, heal up, and off we go! As we prepared for the surgery, once again I was escorted to the waiting room while my mom was rolled away. This time the surgeon accompanied me.

"Nada," he said, looking at me, "This surgery should take four hours because I'll have to put a whole new feeding tube in if it's blocked and knotted up."

"Ok," I said.
"If I come back out in less than an hour, it's the worst-case scenario."

A flash of fear. "What does that mean?" I asked.

"It means the cancer has spread to her stomach, and we can't help her."

I just stared at him. "Okay," I said. "I'll wait here."

I never prayed so hard in all of my life. All I could do was pray and ask God for help, protection, strength, and wisdom to get through the next few hours.

Please save my mom, please save my mom.

I sat there quietly trying to stay calm while my mom was in surgery. Twenty three minutes had gone by, but it felt like a lifetime.

Twenty three minutes had gone by.

Twenty three minutes had gone by, and the doctor came back out.

I lost it. I broke down and cried hysterically once I saw him. The whole waiting room stopped and just stared at me as I wailed in tears holding back nothing. I couldn't believe it, it was the worst day of my life. I was breathing so hard, shaking, and couldn't see straight from all of the makeup pouring down my face and into my eyes.

The doctor sat across from me and with tears in his eyes, said, "I'm sorry."

Crying uncontrollably, I managed to ask, "How long does she have?"

"Less than three months." he replied. "We will need to transfer her to hospice within the next few days, so she can pass comfortably."

I couldn't believe it. From cancer free... to bone cancer with three to five years left... finally, to completely unsaveable with three months left to live.

I couldn't understand. My mind, my heart, and my whole being went numb. At that moment a part of me died.

PRACTICE: Again this story is my own, so take a minute to shake off any feelings that may have emerged as you read it.

- Step 1: Take three deep breaths using your diaphragm; inhale for three, and exhale for three.
- Step 2: Out loud, say one thing that you are incredibly grateful for that has brought fulfillment to your life.
- Use the statement:

I am so incredibly grateful for
_____. Thank you, _____ (insert God, The Universe, Jesus, whatever you acknowledge as a higher power) for blessing me with

_____.

If you have shown gratitude for a person, I encourage you to call them or speak to them in person (not text or email) and express your gratitude.

OUR LAST MOMENTS

Within a few days, my mother and I were headed back home to put her under hospice care. All we could think about was enjoying every second of the day together as a family. My aunts, my mom's sisters flew in, family was over every day, and together we just laughed, talked, and watched our favorite movies. Oh and *General Hospital,* that was a must-watch with my mom.

It was an amazing time, yet incredibly sad. Why do we as human beings wait until it's too late to truly live, love, and embrace the present? Why did it take my mother being diagnosed with terminal cancer to have these moments together? We spend our whole lives being "busy" trying to build "something," and in the meantime, we forget to truly live and embrace the people around us in the current moment.

Although my mother and I had a great relationship before her diagnosis, this newly-found layer of love we found together while she was in hospice was one that we never felt before. It was a deeper bond that we both wanted to cultivate years ago but we just didn't know how.

In the midst of being in hospice care, the Rise Up For You First Annual Conference was quickly approaching. The company had only been running for ten months, but I wanted to throw a conference for my mother to attend and see. At the time no one could imagine that she would be in hospice care unable to walk. I honestly didn't think I was going to make it either as we were two months into hospice and my mom was not doing well. I told my mom that I was going to cancel and not go.

With all of her might, she looked up at me and said, "Nada, you better go! I'll be here when you get back!"

I was scared to leave for fear that she would leave us while I was at the conference. As the founder of the company, I had to be there, and decided to go with prayers that my mom would stay with us. Miraculously, she got a second wind before I left and was even able to watch it live stream from her bed. The event was sold out, which even until today I don't know how I managed to make that happen with divorce and the ups and downs with mom. This is the power and greatness that lies within all of us, but often we don't tap into it until we have reached rock-bottom and have nowhere to go but up.

After the conference I immediately came home, and there she was sitting up in bed smiling and talking, back to her normal self. We talked about the conference and she told me which speakers she liked the best and how proud of me she was. In my heart I was proud as well but felt a sense of relief being back home with her.

THE AWAKENING, LITERALLY

It was November 25th, the day after Thanksgiving and the energy around town was crazy due to Black Friday. My brothers and I were thankful that my mom made it to Thanksgiving. Gratitude and thanks had a whole new meaning, which we had never understood before.

The day went by quickly, and before we knew it, my mother and I were watching our favorite movie, *The*

Last Samurai, with two of my aunts. It was ironic that the movie was on as it created a sense of peace and tranquility in the room. The beauty of life found in the simplest things, the art of being present, and ancient philosophies that surround death are all major themes in the film. We had fun watching the movie together, and I could tell my mom was enjoying it as she always had. As the movie ended, it was getting late, and we were all headed to bed.

I slept with my mom to care for her in the night or to be there when she woke up for her routine swish of the mouth. Over the past five months, my mother would wake up throughout the night every 15 minutes on the dot so she could swish her mouth with some flavored drink. With not being able to eat or drink for the previous nine months, my mother so desperately craved feeling the different flavored liquids in her mouth. She didn't swallow them but simply let them sit in her mouth on her tongue.

As you can imagine I had hit the exhausted-delirious stage months ago from all the 15-minute awakenings each night. Sometimes I would even wake up to my mom saying assertively, "*Nada!*" because I would fall asleep while standing up holding the drink in one hand and a bowl in another.

Sleeping next to my mom was painful, yet it brought a sense of comfort. I knew where she was and I could hear her breathing throughout the night. There were many nights I wanted to burst out in tears, but I couldn't for fear she would hear me. I didn't want her to lose hope and take in my energy, or to lose strength.

I remember it like it was yesterday... After watching *The Last Samurai* and falling asleep right after 10:30, I popped straight up in bed with my heart pounding in my chest and my breath heaving as if I had just run a marathon. I looked down at my Fitbit, thinking I had only been asleep for a few minutes. It was 2:15am. What!!! *2:15!* It had been almost four hours. It had been almost four hours, and my mom didn't wake me up once for her routine drink swish.

I stared straight at the wall in front of me for a minute before calling out, "Mom?"

No answer.

I finally had the courage to turn and look over at my mom. I put my hand on her chest and could see in her eyes that she was gone. People always say that the eyes are the window to the soul. In that moment I knew that it was true, for I could see that my mother was no longer there.

The doctors said that when a patient is coming to the end, their heart rate raises all the way up and then drops instantly. I knew that it had only been a minute or two since she had passed. I believed then and still believe now that my mom's last breath is what knocked the breath out of me, waking me up abruptly.

After sitting with my mom for a minute and crying, I slowly and quietly went downstairs to wake up my older brother. I didn't want anyone else to wake up just yet.

I knocked on his door. "Walid, I need your help. I think she's gone."

He came upstairs with me and confirmed. November 26th, 2016, at approximately 2:10 a.m., a beautiful and graceful soul left its physical form known as Adele Kansao Nasserdeen. She was 63 years old, the same age my father was when he passed. They were together again. Two hearts that loved each other dearly could once again connect in a world and space beyond our human understanding and knowledge.

I will say with full authenticity and openness that the process of losing my mother was traumatic and incredibly painful. ***Most people don't fear death but the way in which they will meet death. (GN #8)*** It's taken me years to get over my anger, and I'm still getting over it, about how she was taken and the hell she had to go through, not only physically but mentally and emotionally. We know that death is inevitable. Sometimes I wish that in that moment I had had the wisdom to allow and accept what life was presenting. However, I recognize that it's easier to do that when it comes to yourself than it is when you're watching another loved one suffer.

The process of losing my mother was so painful—something I will never forget. The actual death of my mother was a personal awakening that I can also never forget or turn my back on. My mother brought me into this world, was there for my first breath when I was a baby, and I had the blessing of being there for her when she took her last breath. Her last moments cracked open my heart and created an awakening within me.

A new life was born!

CHAPTER 2 GOLDEN NUGGETS

As we get older and develop into adults, our parents seem to become more childlike. The circle of life takes effect, and we children begin to take care of our parents as our parents once took care of us.

Most people don't fear death but the way in which they will meet death.

END OF CHAPTER REFLECTIVE QUESTION:

Reflect back onto an experience that has transformed your life. How did it serve you, and what was the lesson it provided?

CHAPTER 3
To Break or To Awaken

CHAPTER 3

Who I am today—with all my strengths and weaknesses, all of my achievements and failures— is a direct result of experience from my past. And in the future, there will be more (perhaps painful) experiences that will ultimately bless me and contribute to my personal growth.

Naturally as human beings, we tend to downplay both our achievements and the pains we've experienced in our lives. We live in a culture that tells us, "Hush, don't tell." We are meant to hide away our pain and vulnerabilities—not just here in America, but throughout the world.

The reality is that everything you have been through up until this point has contributed to who you are in one way or another. For some, their past experience creates an opening and a gratitude for life. For others, their pasts have made them tough and more closed off to emotional experiences or commitment.

In some cases, more extreme, it's given them a life behind bars or living on the streets.

Life, as we know it, is you. You are life. Life is a beautiful journey that is composed with both major and minor chords, augmented and diminished chords. Allow yourself to feel and be in time with the music even when it's not musically pleasing to your ears. And most importantly, ***don't allow anyone to silence the music in you. (GN#9)***

When we go through extreme situations, it's common to start tackling the BIG questions in the aftermath:

- What is the meaning of life?
- What does it mean to be happy?
- How do I live fully and with gratitude?
- Why do these things happen?
- What is God?

After losing my mother, these questions never came to my mind. But one very thought-provoking question did:

*What does it mean to live a life that I am **proud** of?*

This question wouldn't leave my mind. In my heart, I wanted self-assurance that if I died tomorrow, I could say that I lived a life I was proud of. I wanted an inner peace in passing onto the next life, knowing this one wasn't left unlived or taken for granted.

So, what does it mean to live a life that **you** are proud of? What does it look like? How do you get there? Is it all-encompassing or simply limited to your professional accolades?

It is my sincere belief that every experience you go through and continue to go through has led you to where you are today. You may not understand it in the moment. You may not even understand it for years to come, but eventually the truth reveals itself. And in the end, you are grateful for the good, bad, and the ugly that you have endured because it has made you what you are today.

My journey up until this point has led me to two amazing discoveries: one, my purpose is simply to take steps in becoming my best self each and every day, and in the process, inspire others to do the same through love, education, and self-empowerment. And two, I cannot achieve this without taking a direct look into my heart, my soul, my naked self, stripped of everything except my true being. How can I inspire and help others rise if I am not doing the work myself?

The key point here is the realization that positive, *constructive* change and a higher purpose can only manifest when we spark change within ourselves. And when I say *change*, I don't mean the kind of change you conjure up while sitting on the coach, hoping and wishing—but *active* change. Change that gets your hands dirty, knocks you down, and forces you to climb when you think there is nothing left in you.

Let me stop here and say that working on **becoming your best self assumes that there is always greatness within you that is ready to step forward. It does not mean that you are broken and need fixing, but that you are in a constant state of openness, being, and transformation, helping you to continuously RISE. (GN #10)**

I unfortunately learned this the hard way. After the breakdown of things with Amar—and then my mother—I recognized that my sense of self was completely depleted, shaken to its core. My six pillars were suffering drastically, and I was failing. Like a domino effect, after one pillar was in disrepair, they all eventually came crumbling down. If I truly wanted to rise up to become my best self, I had to recognize that nurturing my whole being was necessary.

The movement to Rise Up For You is now. I urge you not to make the same mistake that I and so many others make: sparking change only once you are in a state of desperation or trauma. **Rising up is not limited to picking yourself up when you're at your lowest, but taking yourself higher to reach your next level of potential. (GN#11)**

The number one issue I see with individuals and companies is their lack of commitment to continuous growth when everything seems okay. It's usually the last minute typhoon or the out-of-nowhere earthquake that shakes people to their cores, forcing change and awakening. What if we didn't allow ourselves to fall victims to this fate? What if each and every day we honored and held ourselves to a new standard of greatness and inner potential?

The three P's—potential, preparation, and prevention—are key to reaching the next level toward a fulfilled life.

Potential:
If we are constantly pursuing growth in ourselves, we allow our potential to reach new heights and seek new possibilities. Instead of moving forward from the bottom of the mountain, try moving forward when you're halfway up. The climb is more achievable from there as the peak is almost within your grasp.

Preparation:
When we do the work ahead of time, it allows us to react more efficiently and gracefully when shit hits the fan. All of the work we put in prepares us for moments of uncertainty. We are more centered, more awakened, and more conscious of what needs to be done and how. Not allowing for continuous growth within ourselves stunts our ability to work our

emotional intelligence (EI) muscles, which are key components in building resilience against the unknown.

Prevention:

Lastly, when we do the work before we hit the danger zone, it prevents us from putting ourselves into potentially harmful and unaligned situations. You have the power in you to decide what, where, and how you should live your life. But first you have to honor your life and the power you have within. Constantly nurturing positive change within yourself allows you to become more intuitive and see the big picture when it comes to your purpose, relationships, and overall quality of life.

So again, this is a call out to the world to Rise Up For You now! Not when you're at the bottom and defeated, but while you still have the energy and a clear understanding that your potential is limitless.

PRACTICE: Write a calling, prayer, or message to the universe in your journal and repeat it to yourself everyday. This will empower you to reach new heights and be better than you were yesterday. The power of your words is better recognized when it's called out in a strong, loving, and affirming voice.

Here's the calling I read to myself each and every day, out loud. Mine is specifically noted to God, but that is my personal preference. Your calling does not need to be associated with a higher power of any kind.

> *Dear God,*
> *Thank you for the blessed and awakened life I get to live each day.*
> *Thank you for breath and getting to see another day.*
> *Please help me to help myself to reach my full and greatest potential,*
> *To gain continued clarity in life with Rise Up For You and my calling.*
>
> *God, help me to see my full greatness so that I can help with inspiring and educating myself as well as humanity.*
>
> *Give me the resilience, opportunities, and guidance to become my best self.*
> *I will bring my full self each and every day.*
>
> *Help me to keep my heart open so that I don't miss the love of my life when you bring him to me.*
>
> *I will create and be:*
>
> > *LOVING*
> > *PROSPEROUS*
> > *OPEN HEARTED*
> > *INTENTIONAL*

Money, health, community, love, and success are all here for me.
Transformation, intention, becoming, being, and consumption are my internal laws of being.

God, pour love onto me so that I may always lead and live with love.
I am yours to use for greatness in this lifetime and the next.
Mom, Dad, and Grandma, I love you and thank you for everything.

At the end of the day, we all want greatness for ourselves and our lives. We want happiness, love, abundance, and inner fulfillment.

According to the World Happiness Report, happiness and life satisfaction among United States adolescents, which increased between 1991 and 2011, suddenly declined after 2012 (Twenge et al., 2018a; see Figure 5.2). Thus, by 2016-17, both adults and adolescents were reporting to be significantly less happy than they had been in the previous 25 years or so.

In addition, Meik Wiking, the CEO of the *World Happiness Institute*, states that the following factors are pivotal in building a happy and thriving life:

1. **Take your street and turn it into a community** *(Social and Relationship Management)*. We know that our sense of belonging and togetherness has a big effect on our happiness. Make the effort to speak to your neighbors. Set up a mini-library or a small urban garden, which can be the roots of a strong community.

2. **Build more movement into your daily routine** *(Health and Fitness)*. There are so many more ways to be happy than you think. Take the stairs, have a meeting while going for a walk, or park as far away from the supermarket entrance as possible.

3. **Establish a free-fun fellowship** *(Social and Relationship Management)*. See if you can decouple wealth from well-being. Form a free-fun fellowship with your family or friends where each person takes turns planning an inexpensive activity for the group.

4. **Train your empathy muscles** *(Social and Relationship Management)*. Read a novel, join a charity, or move beyond your normal social circles to get a better understanding of other peoples' behaviors and situations.

5. **Introduce "No Phone Fridays" into your weekly routine**—*or whatever day of the*

week suits you (Social and Relationship Management). If you have kids, you know the challenge of getting them to turn off their devices. In part, this is because all of their friends are on them too. Therefore, try to organize "critical analogue mass" at the local community level—your street or the kids' classmates—where nobody uses their devices for the same period, so they have someone to play with, without the devices.

6. **Start talking about mental health** (Health). Leverage mental health apps to manage your sleep, anxiety, and/or depression. Next time you ask someone how they are doing, take a *real* interest in their answer, and do not accept "*Fine.*" If you are concerned for someone, a question like, "I've been worried about you. Can we talk about what you have been experiencing?" may start the conversation.

7. **Create a greater sense of freedom at work** (Career). Introduce concepts like" quiet Tuesday mornings" at work where you carve out three hours once a week without interruptions—no meetings, no phone calls, no emails, no managers asking for status reports are allowed.

As noted above, social and relationship management (also known as your interactions and connections), financial awareness and management, a purpose-driven profession, loving relationships, and health are all essential components in becoming your best self.

There is one final pillar that has yet to be addressed. But this final pillar is the most important, and without it, sustainability and forward movement cannot exist: *Self-Worth*.

We all naturally thrive in one or two of the six pillars. Some of us are great at building community, others building their careers. In full transparency, my core pillar and strongest suit is self-worth, without which Rise Up For You would have never existed—nor would this book.

A lack of self-worth or the belief that you are incapable/not enough is one of the worst self-fulfilling prophecies humans have manifested. (GN#12) We subject ourselves to awful circumstances, broken relationships, unhealthy environments, all because we don't *honor ourselves* enough to walk away. We miss out on opportunities, lash out at others, and let fear cripple us simply because we do not know the greatness that lies within us—every one of us.

We are all born innocent, pure, and abundantly confident. It is only with time that our circumstances change our beliefs and perspective about who we are, and thus change how we see ourselves. But in that scenario, we have not become any less great. Our minds have simply become clouded by beliefs that do not belong to us, and year after year, we have become increasingly paralyzed because of it.

Around the world I have seen this infectious disease cloud the minds of young children, adults, and successful professionals from all walks of life. All of us will at one point or another be affected by a lack of self-worth and broken confidence. We should work together and make a conscious effort to break this vicious cycle, within ourselves and around ourselves. The journey to become your best self starts right here with this first pillar: *Self-Worth.*

Let me start by saying that self-worth is a daily practice. There will be days when you don't have it, and days when you have an abundance of it. Accepting this with compassion is a part of developing your sense of self-worth and is needed in your everyday journey. There are a number of factors that can tear down your self-worth, which is why it needs to be constantly nurtured. One day you might feel amazing, and the next day a loved one will say or do something that causes you to question your whole being and whether or not you are good enough.

In years of study and working with thousands of youth and adults, I have come to know four major contributors to a lack of self-worth and confidence. Please note that the percentages assigned are anecdotal, formed from the years I spent working with individuals on developing their confidence.

We asked over 200 men and women what affected their confidence most. Here's what they replied.

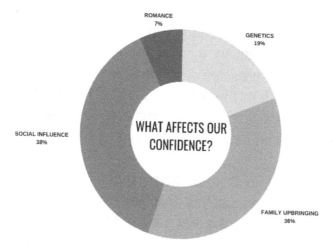

Genetic Make-up:

In the past, research has not traditionally supported the notion that confidence is genetic. However, studies have shown that variants of the OXTR gene (the receptor for oxytocin, which is the hormone that produces positive emotion) may be linked to stress-related traits and other psychological patterns.

A number of scientists at UCLA conducted a study, asking over 300 volunteers to complete questionnaires measuring three psychological resources and assessing any symptoms of depression.

Their results suggested that people who have one or two copies of the OXTR gene with an *A* (adenine) *allele* at a particular location tended to have more negative measurements than those with two copies of the *G* (guanine) *allele*. People with an *A allele* were less optimistic, had lower self-esteem, and felt less personal mastery than people with two *G alleles*. In addition, the *A allele* was linked to higher levels of depressive symptoms. Follow-up analyses suggest that the effects of OXTR variants on depression are largely mediated by the gene's influence on psychological resources.

The gene itself is far from completely dominating one's confidence, but it is important to note that genetics is a factor that can lead to low self-worth if external factors do not counterbalance the impact.

Romantic Partners:

Human beings are meant to love and be loved. It is one of the most painful yet gratifying feelings we can experience. When love is great, we feel on top of the world, but when it's bad, life can feel torturous.

Because romance has such a profound cognitive, emotional, and physical power over us, the effects of our relationships can be long-lasting and perhaps detrimental to our future, potential romantic partners. Everything said and done in the course of our relationships has the power to hit us ten times harder than if it were a friend or family member. Romantic love makes us punch drunk and often leaves us in extreme states of being.

Everything is in circular movement until we decide to break the pattern. Hurt people hurt others, and therefore unfortunately, it is inevitable that we all encounter heartbreak at some point in our lives. It might come in the form of abuse from a partner, whether it's mental, verbal, financial, physical, or sexual. But sometimes the heartbreak is simply a result of a disintegrating relationship without really understanding *why*.

The hardest part about losing a loved one is doing the playback of the relationship in your mind and questioning "Was it ever real? Did the things they said actually have truth behind them?" Everyone does this when they are the ones who are broken up with or hurt in the name of love. A broken heart is one of the most difficult situations to rebound from and for some, it can stay with them for a lifetime.

We consciously and subconsciously take our wounds and barriers with us from one relationship to the next. In some cases we even sabotage new relationships that could be going great for fear that one day it will fall apart. Projecting our past pain onto others is the perfect recipe for disaster in a relationship.

The accumulated heartbreak we have endured or the guilt from the hearts we've broken ourselves can break down our confidence in every way. Because relationships are threefold—embodying mental, emotional, and physical connections—we naturally lose confidence in every aspect of ourselves when our hearts are broken. We may come to question our beauty, intelligence, sexual capability, or our very ability to love—literally *everything* we are as a person can be questioned and torn down in our minds.

Then of course, the loss of physical connection when a relationship dissolves can cause people to feel like addicts detoxing from the highs of physical touch. Research has shown that sex releases dopamine in your body, which is similar to the effects of drugs and rock and roll, creating a feeling of withdrawal once it is gone.

Although romance is a significant component in the makeup of an individual's confidence, it's not a *necessary* factor if the other areas of one's life have set them up for success.

Family Upbringing:

Coming from a positive and supportive upbringing, for example, plays a larger role in the development and sustainment of confidence. And in fact, the more confidence we are able to develop before romantic relationships come into play, the better we are able to navigate through eventual heartbreak without letting it destroy our self-worth and future relationships.

We are all born unstoppable! Remember back to when you were a child, or if you have children yourself, remember their childhood when they were between the ages of 2-7. There is a wild and curious spirit at this age that has no limitations or understanding of the concept "I can't." Most young children think they are invincible, which is evident from the plethora of videos on social media of parents intercepting their kids from jumping off couches, touching burning hot stoves, and saving them from other mortal dangers.

Over time, these open children become more and more limited and influenced by those around them. Parents, siblings, other family members, and outside influences begin to teach and assimilate children to model the acceptable behaviors of our society and culture—both positive and negative. Research on child development shows that from infancy, the human brain is gathering data at an incredible rate.

Learning begins prenatally, and children are not only "ready to learn" but already actively learning from the time they are born. From birth, a child's mind is active and inquisitive, and early thinking is insightful and complex. Many of the foundations of sophisticated forms of learning, including those important to academic success, are established in the earliest years of life.

Development and early learning can be supported continuously as a child develops, and early knowledge and skills inform and influence future learning. When adults understand how the mind develops, what progress children make in their cognitive abilities, and how active inquiry and learning are children's natural inclination, they can foster cognitive growth by supporting children's active engagement with new experiences and providing developmentally appropriate stimulation of new learning through responsive, secure, and sustained caregiving relationships.

The key issue is that we are living in circular motion. As adults we hardly take the time to work on our personal challenges or limiting beliefs; and in turn, we pass our pain, habits, and beliefs on to our children, creating a circular effect of mental stigmas. *Every time we say no without an explanation, use negative reinforcement, pass down our beliefs consciously or subconsciously, we are influencing young minds and either setting them up for success or creating barriers in their minds mentally that may last for years or a lifetime. (GN#13)* Divorce, abuse in any form, parental insecurities, poor communication, and absent parenting are just a few elements that dramatically affect the upbringing of a child and who they become.

I speak from experience here. My siblings and I all maintain an uncanny confidence and self-worth that has propelled us forward in our relationships, careers, and life experiences. In trying to understand where that sense of self-worth and confidence comes from, I can't help but examine the steps our parents took, which made a huge impact on who we are today. Here are a few things I remember from my childhood that undoubtedly made a difference:

Positive Affirmations: As my mother drove us to school every day, she would have us repeat positive affirmations in the car: "Today, I'm going to put my best foot forward. I am smart. Thank you, God, for allowing us to see another day. I will study hard, be kind, and I won't be afraid to ask questions."

These reinforcements were so ingrained in my head that when a teacher (the people that spend equal if not more time with you during your adolescence) told me I couldn't do something or put me down, I wouldn't hear them and most times countered back and stuck up for myself.

Sports: My parents put all three of us—my brothers and me—in sports, starting at a young age. Not only did they do it to keep us active and socially connected with other kids, but most importantly, they wanted us to understand failure—and that failure is sometimes possible even after weeks or months of practice. Not every game ended in victory, and sometimes we hardly played. But working to strengthen the muscle that handles failure, even after working hard, taught us how to be resilient and to try again. Failure no longer became a scary thing, but a challenge. Not trying and putting our best foot forward was what became scary to us.

A Constant Push for Ourselves: I would be lying if I said my father wasn't hard on us—he was. He was a Lebanese immigrant who came to the United States with $22 in his pocket. He built a life from the ground up with hardly any English-speaking skills in the beginning. My father did not understand the words "I can't." Furthermore, he didn't understand working hard _for someone else_.

He was here alone, and all of his hard work and determination was for himself because deep down he honored himself enough to know that he deserved greatness. My father, Nabih Nasserdeen, pushed my brothers and me beyond what we thought our limits were, but he never suggested that we do it for him—or anyone else for that matter. His main motto throughout our childhood was: "Nobody is better than you, and you are no better than anyone else. You have nothing to prove to anyone, except you." In short, if we had the capability to do something, why not put our best foot forward and do it? Nobody was going to do it for us, especially not our parents!

I remember once asking my dad if he was proud of me. His response was, "I am proud. But it is not whether I am proud of you, but whether *you* are proud of you." **I think indirectly he was teaching us that people come and go in your life, and the only constant is your relationship with yourself. (GN#14)** If you nurture that idea and hold true to it, you will always have the will to be your best self.

Present Parenting: At the end of the day, we respected and listened to our parents—not because of their roles as "mother and father," but because they *walked the walk*. They were kind, worked hard, made time for themselves, and showed up 100% of the time. On top of that they made time for us children. No matter how stressed out my parents were about money, financial up and downs, or family-related issues, our parents always played with us and engaged in meaningful conversations even when we were little kids. The importance of truly interacting with and understanding your children is an underrepresented idea in our society today.

Developing those strong family ties and understanding caused us kids to be more receptive when we got in trouble. It's because we respected our parents and knew that they cared about us as individuals. They didn't just show up and tell us what to do; they built a relationship with us so that when they did tell us what to do, we wanted to listen and valued their guidance. The beautiful thing is that as we got older the tables reversed and soon they valued the opinions and guidance we gave to them as adults.

Influencing children and being a parent is the most honorable job a person can have, and yet this monumental responsibility is often taken on without much forethought. Have we forgotten that the next leaders, presidents, and world influencers are the children we are currently raising? Most of who you are today is because of what you experienced from infancy to adolescence (or when you became a young adult). If a strong foundation is built at a younger age, a young adult is less likely to accept limiting or damaging beliefs that are cast upon them by society.

Currently, as I write this section of the book, I'm traveling through Scandinavia (Denmark, Norway, and Sweden). What I have witnessed here between parents and their children is something I have never seen in all my travels. The nurturing and love that exudes from both parents is as authentic, loving, and as comforting as it gets. I have seen more men in suits carrying babies on their chest as they walk down the street without their wives to be found, more parents cuddling with their children and laughing with them as if they were longtime friends, and you won't believe me when I say this, but I have yet to see one child under the age of ten years old with a mobile phone or iPad in their hand. The parent-child connection here is one that seems unaffected by today's modern technology and fast-paced lifestyle. This well-maintained connection between parents and their children contributes to the mental health and well-being of the Scandanavian youth and their rising generation today.

Social Influence While Growing Up:

It would be irresponsible to claim that parenting is the sole contributor in the building of a person's self-worth. The truth is there are multiple sources of influence that parents cannot control.

Today—particularly with the prevalence of social media, cyber-bullying, influencers, bloggers, and reality TV—the "comparison game" and all the varying definitions of who we should and should not be are out of control. We as individuals are constantly consuming ideas, thoughts, and principles at an astonishing rate—all of which directly impacts how we feel about ourselves, who we are becoming, and how we treat others. The mass media has no control over content, and more and more we are becoming disconnected from truth and infatuated with a fantasy life.

Current research demonstrates that the increase in depression and suicide for both young people and adults has been attributed to the use of (and social importance assigned to) social media and online networking. The apparent ease and accessibility to *compare* oneself to what society says is the "gold standard" is present everywhere. Self-worth has become dependent on the amount of likes and comments one receives on a post. The dopamine in our minds is being triggered less and less by love and real human connection, and instead, is being triggered by the intrigue and the false sense of acceptance the online world provides.

The worst part is that this new "social media/digital influencing" manifests into our behavior and how we socialize with others. Everything we see online, whether good or bad, gives us permission to act in the same way. Violence, hatred, bigotry, and the ability to publicly complain about another person instead of communicating and resolving things with them directly, have all heightened our abilities to trust and connect. We are collectively living in fear, judgment, and self-deprivation.

When we lack fulfillment and are consumed with hurt and fear, it is all we have to pass down to others. (GN#15) Every interaction—whether it is teacher to a student or a cashier to a customer—offers the possibility to influence someone, and yet many of us show no regard, understanding, or care for how we use that influence. All of these small, interactive moments, along with larger more substantial social connections, play a role in how we conceive of ourselves. Consider all the peers, teachers, and co-workers who have influenced you both positively or negatively over the course of your life.

Rebuilding Our Self-Worth

Building your self-worth and confidence goes beyond bubble baths and spa days— although those are some of the best ways to treat yourself in creating instant relaxation. What's important to emphasize here is that confidence and self-worth are the key stepping stones to building your whole life. *Self-worth is the key to sustainable success! (GN#16)*

The latest research shows that professional and personal success are tied more closely to the confidence you have in yourself, not the technique you accumulate over time. Also *emotional intelligence* (EI) appears to be a key indicator in success today, and the first two quadrants (as defined by EI pioneer himself, Daniel Goleman) self-awareness and self-management are focused on the confidence, resilience, and thoughts we have about ourselves.

The biggest mistake we make as individuals along this journey is thinking that the work is only done here and there or when in need. In actuality the work should and needs to be done every day. The deep *inner* work, not the surface work that is portrayed on social media with quotes, massages, and wine nights—the deep work.

The question is: "If everything was stripped from you—your career, your clothes, all of your belongings and money, even the very roof over your head—who would you be, and would you be happy with yourself?" The sad truth is that so many of us don't know the answer to this question, which is why the suicide rate in America has skyrocketed. Every individual, regardless of social class or economic status, knows what it feels like to fall short—to feel like you are not enough. And when tough times come—losing a job, divorce, financial stress, or as we speak, COVID19 — the only answer that seems fitting for some is to take their own life.

"numerous indicators of low psychological well-being such as depression, suicidal ideation, and self-harm increased sharply among adolescents since 2010, particularly among girls and young women (Mercado et al., 2017; Mojtabai et al., 2016; Plemmons et al., 2018; Twenge et al., 2018b, 2019a)...

This decline in happiness and mental health seems paradoxical. By most accounts, Americans should be happier now than ever. The violent crime rate is low, as is the unemployment rate. Income per capita has steadily grown over the last few decades. This is the Easterlin paradox: As the standard of living improves, so should happiness – but it has not.

Several credible explanations have been posited to explain the decline in happiness among adult Americans, including declines in social capital and social support (Sachs, 2017) and increases in obesity and substance abuse (Sachs, 2018)."

We currently live in a society where worth is determined by our belongings, our job titles, and the kinds of cars we drive. Our mental health is suffering at the hands of government policies, irresponsible behavior, social media influence, and the persistent bombardment of news and media, which all tell us how to live, what to value, and ultimately causes us to consume ourselves with the fear of never being or having enough.

It's time to re-write these standards for the sake of humanity and step into our full potential on our own terms. (GN#17) The time to make a change within ourselves starts today, not tomorrow, not in a year, but now in this current moment as you read the lines of this chapter.

CHAPTER 3 GOLDEN NUGGETS

….don't allow anyone to silence the music in you.

Becoming your best self assumes that there is always greatness within you that is ready to step forward. It does not mean that you are broken and need fixing, but that you are in a constant state of openness, being, and transformation, helping you to continuously RISE.

Rising up is not limited to picking yourself up when you're at your lowest, but taking yourself higher to reach your next level of potential.

A lack of self-worth or the belief that you are incapable/not enough is one of the worst self-fulfilling prophecies humans have manifested.

Every time we say no without an explanation, use negative reinforcement, pass down our beliefs consciously or subconsciously, we are influencing young minds and either setting them up for success or creating barriers in their minds mentally that may last for years or a lifetime.

I think indirectly he was teaching us that people come and go in your life, and the only constant is your relationship with yourself.

When we lack fulfillment and are consumed with hurt and fear, it is all we have to pass down to others.

Self-worth is the key to sustainable success!

It's time to re-write these standards for the sake of humanity and step into our full potential on our own terms.

END OF CHAPTER REFLECTIVE QUESTION:

Write down three things that you are proud of, which have nothing to do with your profession, your skills, or your belongings. Dig deep and remember to ask yourself: if you were stripped of all external titles and achievements, who are you? What would you be proud of?

_____

_____

_____

_____

_____

CHAPTER 4
Let's Talk Confidence

CHAPTER 4

I remember one time I was speaking at a women's juvenile detention center to an audience of young ladies, ages 14-21. Some of these young women had been caught up in prostitution and trafficking, but some of them had committed murder—these were teenagers, mind you.

As I was speaking, I remember saying with confidence and pride, "I want you to be confident, love yourself, and recognize that your life is not over. You can overcome your current circumstance."

I vividly remember a young lady shouting back, "I don't want to be confident! Why? So I can be told I am a b—ch?"

Whoa! Her words stopped me dead in my tracks. I looked at her and asked, "Who told you that's what confidence is?"

For the next fifteen minutes, I preached about confidence and loving yourself as if my life depended on it! If that was my last day on earth, I needed these young women to know that confidence is one thing you should not turn away from.

The term confidence has been beaten up and distorted by a number of insufficient and inaccurate definitions. With all of the science-based research to back up its importance, there still seems to be a misunderstanding of what it truly means and why we as individuals need to take the time to nurture this skill in abundance. Let's first start by stating what confidence is not.

Confidence is not:
- A mean, bitchy, or stuck-up attitude towards others.
- An exaggeration of your achievements and abilities.
- Putting others down so that you can advance.
- Limited to only your skill and technique.
- Speaking up at every chance you get just to be heard.
- Walking away from tough or challenging situations with people because you're just too good for them (This excludes extreme situations involving violence, abuse, or influences that have a detrimental effect on your well-being).

- Being alone and taking challenges on by yourself when you could use a hand or support.

Just to be clear, since there has been a notable shift in society when it comes to confidence, the definition from the *Merriam-Webster Dictionary* describes confidence as:
- A feeling or consciousness of one's powers or of reliance on one's circumstances
- Faith or belief that one will act in a right, proper, or effective way
- The quality or state of being certain
- Relation of trust or intimacy

For the sake of our discussion here, let's define confidence as:
- An inner belief that one can learn and build a given skill or technique with hard work and commitment—associated with having a growth mindset
- Allowing yourself to take risks
- Not seeking failure, but graciously accepting failure if and when it occurs
- Having a resilience that enables you to keep trying even when you encounter challenges and shortcomings
- Admitting when you don't know something and having a willingness to learn
- Pure kindness and openness toward others

- Speaking up in times of need to add value, contribute, and support
- Sticking up for yourself and others when some wrongdoing has occurred
- Knowing when to walk away from a situation for protection of yourself and loved ones
- A trust and love in yourself that can be bruised, but will not be broken by others
- Understanding your worth and not accepting anything less in your career, relationships, and life decisions

There are two types of confidence: outer and inner. Both types are crucial in building your overall confidence; however, the inner confidence takes longer to cultivate and is a constant work in progress. The outer confidence, however, is more apparent and noticeable to others. But don't let this fool you! A person can seem like they have a lot of confidence because they have mastered the outer, but someone who displays a healthy outer confidence doesn't necessarily mean they are a truly confident person.

Outer confidence can be classified as the following:

Your posture and how you carry yourself physically - Walking tall with your shoulders back and head upwards. Avoiding a slouched posture and staring at the floor.

Eye contact - Looking others in the eye instead of constantly shifting your eyes up, down, and to the side as if something in the sky is trying to tell you something.

Appearing "put together" - Do you take the time to honor yourself and the way you show up in the world? Yes, putting yourself together—such as doing your hair, dressing appropriately for occasions, and showing up with a bright and an awakened face—communicates to the people around you a lot about how you feel about yourself.

Non-verbal cues - What messages are you communicating with your non-verbal cues? Are you open in your posture while people talk to you, or do you close yourself off with folded arms? Having an open presence can relay great confidence in yourself as well as bring out openness and outer confidence in others.

Energy - The energy that you exude instantly lets a person know how you feel about yourself and others. Smiling often, showing you care when others are speaking, and maintaining a persistent enthusiasm are all clear signs that your internal compass is on the right track.

Nothing is more attractive than confidence! I'm not talking about just outer confidence, but inner confidence as well. The sad truth is that many of us lack true confidence—confidence that allows us to take risks, be ourselves, and truly live a happy and fulfilled life. Every step we take or choose not to take is due to our level of confidence and the beliefs we have about ourselves. But know that **everything you will ever need is already inside of you; it's time for you to uncover all of the gold that has been buried under the rubble. (GN #18)**

Your confidence is already inside you, and it's stronger and more needed than you think. Everyone needs confidence and we all struggle from a lack of it at one point or another during our lives. You can be confident in a particular skill. You can also be confident in some areas of your life and less in others.

Let me tell you, the first time I spoke on stage I was freaking out! Even though I had sung and performed in front of thousands of people already, I wasn't confident in public speaking yet. I was shaking, going through the imposter syndrome, and thinking, "Who am I to be up here?" But that didn't stop me! That fear and lack of confidence was in my car, but I did not let it take the wheel!

You may be reading this thinking: "I am incredibly confident in my career and professional relationships." You're successful, move up the career ladder, and have no problem speaking up in a professional environment. But perhaps you are lacking confidence in your love life. Perhaps you haven't met the right partner and over time that has made you feel unlovable, messing with your confidence to connect with a romantic partner. This is what I like to call *Macro- and Micro-confidence.*

- *Micro-confidence: a belief in yourself as it relates to one particular area, skill or competency. You are a confident singer, or perhaps confident in your job role. This level of confidence is not sustainable and is constantly shifting.*
- *Macro-confidence: a deep-rooted belief in oneself that you can and will overcome, achieve and make the proper decisions for yourself and your future success. This level of confidence is sustainable and transferable in any job, relationship, life experience, etc. The Macro level gives you the confidence and belief to build more micro confidence. For example, learning a new skill, being adaptable, making the ask.*

It's important to cultivate the Macro level of confidence for sustainable success and fulfillment. At this current moment in time, the COVID-19 pandemic continues to affect all our lives in drastic ways, and many people have lost their sense of identity and worth through this experience. Why? Because their *micro-confidence* factors have shifted, been taken away for a limited time, or have completely dissolved altogether. People who were once confident in their career are now jobless—people confident in owning their business, now shutting doors—confident in their relationships, now on the way to divorce. Micro-confidence is not sustainable. It's the extra cherry on top once you have cultivated confidence on the macro level.

I'll pause here and say that rebuilding your confidence and self-worth is not something that happens overnight. I want to be transparent in saying this because we live in a "quick-fix" society, which demands everything immediately without putting in all the time and requisite work. *The journey to becoming your best self is a lifelong commitment, and unless you're ready for it, you will continue to live life as an up-and-down roller coaster. (GN#19)*

Your confidence is already inside you, but it has been wounded and pushed down by your past experiences—regardless of how traumatic or insignificant you think they are. Every experience you have had so far—both positive and negative—has affected your belief system, which is directly related to your confidence. The most important thing in building your confidence, your career, and your overall success is understanding that the only person who can change what you feel and how you move forward is you. A new relationship, a house, car, a new job, these things can distract you from your feelings. *No other person, no material possession, no activity can remove, release, or change how you feel and give you lasting self-worth. (GN#20)*

How often do you hear people say things like, "When I lose weight, I'll feel super confident!" Or, "When I'm married, I won't feel lonely anymore." We take our feelings with us wherever we go, in every relationship, job, and step we take. We can't run away from them—they follow us until we face them.

Studies show that your childhood environment and experiences from infancy to young adulthood play a huge role in how you feel and think about yourself. If your childhood was filled with hurt, abuse, derogatory comments, or bullying, it may have resulted in self-hatred, negative self-talk, and self-doubt.

Here are some contributing factors to low confidence and self-worth:
- Limitations or beliefs passed down from your parents
- Words of hurt or doubt expressed to you by loved ones
- The behavior of teachers and the way they made you feel
- Past romantic relationships
- Your environment in general
- Friends—their attitude and energy

- Significant experiences that scarred you
- Any form of abuse
- Extreme life situations: divorce, rape, illness, poverty, death
- A lack of personal and professional support
- Negative social interaction with peers: bullying, harassment, isolation

If these circumstances aren't properly dealt with through self-healing, guide therapy, or mentorship, a lifetime of struggling and inner conflict can result. **The more time we go without resolution and doing the inner work, the more we *become* our past experiences. (GN #21)** Our past feelings, thoughts, and scars become who we are and become our very identity. We become our thoughts, story, and past wounds.

As a society, we very rarely promote the awareness and understanding of internal and external issues. Most people try to push any hurt or pain down to the bottom of their feet; they try to forget certain things ever happened, or they will say, "Oh well. No big deal" (but not really mean it).

All of these acts of self-preservation create *dis*-ease. These issues never really go away but manifest in your body as some form of pain or another. Before you know it something or someone brings it right back up to the surface. Your body becomes full of toxins that you have accumulated throughout your life that do not serve you. You feel stuck in your self-doubt and lack confidence because somewhere along your journey, you had an experience where you felt that and didn't deal with it.

The following are a few examples, from MK Projects, of the methods people use to avoid feeling and dealing with their emotions:

- Ignoring your feelings/pretending something hasn't happened
- Overeating eating foods loaded with fat and sugar
- Exercising compulsively
- Any type of compulsive behavior
- Always keeping busy—not allowing yourself to feel
- Constant intellectualizing and analyzing
- Working excessively
- Keeping conversations superficial
- Burying angry emotions under a mask of inauthentic peace and love
- Avoiding social environments and networking events
- Drug or alcohol abuse
- Extreme sexual activity with no emotion or connection
- Constant socializing and FOMO (Fear of Missing Out)

PRACTICE: This may be a tough one for you, but take some time to go through the list from MK Projects and identify any points that are true for you. Let's start the deep dive and begin to understand in what form your experiences have manifested. I'll be transparent and share that "Always keeping busy so that I don't have time to feel or think," is a pattern that occasionally creeps up for me.

I know it can be tough to go down the list and identify which patterns may have become manifest in your life, but don't worry. You're not alone! In a recent study by the Rise Up For You Team, we asked over 350 working professionals—from Fortune 500 executives to self-employed entrepreneurs—a series of 60 Emotional Intelligence questions associated with mindset, confidence, and leadership to better understand their career weaknesses and strengths. 75% of respondents answered that the #1 challenge they had all tied into confidence. Advocating for yourself, overcoming self-doubt, motivation to be better, and making the ask—all things directly related to confidence! 52% of professionals actually used the term "more confidence."

The great news is: confidence is a skill that can be learned! Even the genetic factor can be overruled if you can set yourself up for success in the right environment and with the right tools. As Abigail

Barronian says in *The Science Behind the Confidence Gap*, "The receptor-genes that handle dopamine and oxytocin—two other neurotransmitters linked to confidence—also come in similar variations, further ensuring genetics' role in confidence. An important note: having the less favorable version of these genes does not sentence you to a life of anxiety. Nurture—your experiences, your upbringing, and your decision to seek out confidence—has a huge role to play in this as well."

Wherever the gap in confidence lies, we can bridge it! Getting back to the core of confidence is key and a major element in the journey to becoming your best self and closing the gap between you and your potential. Love, fulfillment, and happiness are all yours. Life is too short to go through this journey of life without it so let's take a stand now and together get back to the C.O.R.E of who we are.

CHAPTER 4 GOLDEN NUGGETS

Everything you will ever need is already inside of you; it's time for you to uncover all of the gold that has been buried under the rubble.

The journey to becoming your best self is a lifelong commitment, and unless you're ready for it, you will continue to live life as an up-and-down roller coaster.

No other person, no material possession, no activity can remove, release, or change how you feel and give you lasting self-worth.

The more time we go without resolution and doing the inner work, the more we become our past experiences.

END OF CHAPTER REFLECTIVE QUESTION:

Make a micro list of all the things you are confident in today. Remember Micro means skills, competencies, or certain areas of your life that you feel fully confident in. Now make a list of things that you do not feel confident in that are hindering your overall success and fulfillment. Which list is most important to you? How do you feel about what you wrote down?

_____

_____

_____

_____

_____

_____

CHAPTER 5
Getting Back to C.O.R.E.^{2}

CHAPTER 5

Getting back to the core of who you are is essential as you strive to become the best version of yourself. Through all of my experiences coaching and mentoring, my time as a professional C-Suite executive, and personal in-depth study, I have come to the conclusion that your confidence lies in your C.O.R.E.^{2} (or "core-squared")

C.O.R.E^2 is a method I have developed to help individuals regain their confidence in a strategic, yet loving way. Although some of the principles aren't new to the field, the accumulated curriculum of C.O.R.E^2 has never been delivered in this manner. Cutting-edge research by psychologists like Martin Seligman, Elizabeth Gilbert, and Adam Grant—just to name a few—are taking the field of Positive Psychology by storm, generating conversation around what it means to be resilient, optimistic, and mindful.

However, among that research it appears the topic of confidence has yet to be fleshed out in a meaningful way. And yet ***getting back to the core of confidence and how to build confidence are stepping stones in strengthening your self-worth, rising up for you, and ultimately closing the gap in your potential. (GN#22)***

The C.O.R.E² Method comprises five essential steps to help rebuild confidence and self-worth in yourself. I take a deep dive into each of the steps while providing you an opportunity for reflection, application, and self-empowerment.

> C - Compassion (for yourself)
> O - Optimism (that's realistic)
> R - Reverse Engineering
> E² - Emotional Intelligence
> E² - Enoughism

Compassion for Yourself

Look, I'm going to be completely transparent here and say that the word "self-help" and the personal and professional growth space makes me cringe at times. I realize my saying this may seem comical considering this is the industry I have chosen to dedicate my life to—and I continue to invest many hours of my own personal and professional development. But just like every industry, you have great scholars and pioneers who are doing great work, positively impacting others and changing lives. And then there are others who are capitalizing on other peoples' pain, fears, and tragedies.

To start with, *the word self-help indicates your self is in need of help, and while that may be the case, growth shouldn't necessarily stem from needing or wanting help. It can stem simply because you'd like to bloom into a greater version of yourself. (GN#23)*

Also, there are a series of stigmas and sometimes aggressive messaging tied to the self-help industry. Have you ever seen the Facebook and Instagram videos that say, "You just gotta do it, you have to be motivated. You just have to! Go now and do it! Don't waste your time and don't waste mine. If you want to succeed and make millions, you just have to put your mind to it!" Now, I'm not degrading anyone or any program, but the challenge with some of this messaging is that it can make the targeted audience feel bad about themselves if they choose not wake up at 4am to work out, for example—or if they fail in hitting goals they set for themselves. So many people who are investing in their growth and trying to build a positive, motivating mindset are also beating themselves up every time they make a mistake or discover a shortcoming.

We have built a billion-dollar industry that in some ways makes us feel bad when we don't jump up and down to buy a $30,000 program! How does that work? Again, I'm not putting down the industry as I am also in it—but I have seen people in need of mentorship, new tools, and to get their business going from the ground up. And when they didn't spend $25,000 on a coaching program because they couldn't afford it, they were meant to feel bad in front of a whole room full of people who did buy in.

I share this story and my thoughts to say that the journey is tough! You will fall, you will fail, and you will have shortcomings—over and over again. And if you don't have *compassion* for yourself when these obstacles present themselves, you will continue to mentally torture yourself.

Compassion is a beautiful word. It means to respond and relate to someone who has suffered or feels pain—showing kindness and support to those in need. Compassion for yourself means acting in the same way, but toward yourself as you go through difficult times or fail.

When we have compassion for others we are able to see that they are human, and we understand that no one is perfect. (GN #24) Having compassion for yourself brings humanity to the forefront and allows you to recognize that you are not a robot and that mistakes are inevitable as a human being. It allows you to put yourself on the same level as the rest of humanity.

When we lack compassion for ourselves, our relationships with others and ourselves suffer. *If we can't show kindness and love to ourselves, can we really show it to others? (GN#25)* Rather than feeling unworthy when we fall or show up below our best, self-compassion allows us to uphold our self-worth. When we practice compassion for ourselves, we are no longer reliant on others to tell us that we're okay and deserving because we know it ourselves already. Compassion for yourself is a precursor to resilience, which we will dive into later in this chapter.

Martin Seligman conducted a study on the general happiness of people in an attempt to discover what the key differences were between happy and unhappy people. His studies show that happier people didn't necessarily make more money, look a certain way, or have booming careers; in fact, happier people had great social relationships and also had great relationships with themselves. Our thoughts especially directed towards ourselves affect our well-being, and Martin Seligman's research stands behind it. And to be fair, it's possible to have a great relationship with yourself while still having moments where you lack compassion towards yourself.

This is a journey for me as well. There are moments where I beat myself up about the relationship between my mom and me, especially in her later years. As much as we loved each other, moments of anger at myself still pop-up because I wish I had been more gentle, more loving, and more kind to her in every way. I wish that I hadn't been so stubborn, so strict, and so bothered by her when deep down inside I knew it was an attempt to just get more love from her kids.

So the question that so many of us ask is *how*? How do we create and build self-compassion? Building these human skills aka soft skills isn't as cut and dry as building hard skills. Learning how to work an excel sheet or doing math is a technical skill that doesn't require much emotional work. Developing self-compassion takes a lot of unseen work that for some won't be felt or seen for years to come. That may sound discouraging, but trust me—every small step you take will make a world of a difference for you as long as you are patient. Here are a few of the top practices for building self-compassion.

ROLE PLAY - What Would You Say?

Imagine you have a big project at work which many of your co-workers are dependent on. During your project, a shortcoming or error occurred that affected everyone. You feel terrible, embarrassed, and ashamed that you made such a big mistake.
Your thoughts after the error was revealed might be something like: "I didn't do well on the project everybody was counting on. I'm not equipped for this

job. I let everyone down!" This is the typical kind of self-talk we usually have with ourselves—critical and unforgiving.

Now imagine the same situation happening to the following people in your life. What would you say to them? And is it the same language you would use with yourself?

- What would you say if it were your child?
- What would you say if it were your best friend?
- ...your lover whom you absolutely adore?
- ...your aging parents who have limited time with you?

Here are three principles to remind yourself of when lacking self- compassion:

1. Imperfection That Serves You
How has being imperfect and making mistakes served me positively in the past?

2. Seek Counsel - You're Not The Only One!
Ask friends and mentors for guidance and advice when you fall or make a mistake that you can't seem to get over.

3. No Sideline Critics, Only Helping Hands Allowed
Your thoughts are sideline critics with no guidance.

"Only thoughts with solutions may enter the mind."

Optimism That Is Realistic

As we work toward regaining our confidence, it's important to understand that there will absolutely be bumps in the road. No path is a straight line. Most times, the path is curvy with rocks all over the place, patches of rain, and mudslides. The beautiful thing about life is that we always have a choice. Although our choices might not always be what we want them to be, at the end of the day, how we move forward and how we see the world is in our hands. This is where optimism comes in.

Every moment of life is shaded by our own perspectives and outlooks. Sometimes the shade is grey; other times, it's rosy pink. According to recent research and the leading positive psychologist Martin Seligman, optimism is a key factor in feeling happy, which can lead to greater confidence and less depression. The way we see the world determines how we take action and move forward. If we think there's no chance at the job promotion and lean towards being pessimistic, our self doubt sabotages things, and we won't go after the opportunity. If we think love sucks and we'll never be happily in love, then we will attract partners who will never make us happy.

How we view the world and our own life situations is a key indicator of our ability to *take action*, which goes hand-in-hand with *being confident*. Action is the result of confidence, and optimism allows us to look at the bright side of things—to see the possibility and potential, encouraging us to try again and again.

Let's discuss the difference between optimism and pessimism. Optimism is seeing a situation as temporary. It's recognizing that the state of being or situation is not a fixed state, but is due to outside circumstances, temporary, and only pertinent in that situation and time. Optimism contributes to your self-worth, confidence, overall well-being, and health.

A study examined the optimism of first-year law students in correspondence with their immune response. What they found was that when students were more optimistic, their immune systems had a boost in cell-mediated immunity—the immune cells that respond and fight against foreign viruses and bacteria.

In addition, American suicide and depressions rates among young people and adults are at an all-time high. How is it that a nation with more money, power, and resources, than ever before also has the highest depression rates ever? Optimism done right can be the new medicine that builds our confidence and helps us regain our self-worth and overall happiness.

Pessimists blame themselves for any unfortunate occurrences that happen in their lives. They believe that the cause is a fixed state and if anything positive does happen, it's because of luck. Over time pessimists can develop a learned helplessness where coping mechanisms and resilience become less inherent when faced with adversity and tough situations.

According to an article on Positive Psychology by Elaine Houston, she writes, "Individuals with pessimistic explanatory styles are more likely to experience pervasive and chronic symptoms of helplessness when faced with uncontrollable negative events." In addition, pessimism can contribute to depression and escalate negative thoughts that lead to a circular pattern of learned helplessness and a lack of resilience and grit.

Martin Seligman, the author of *Learned Optimism: How to Change Your Mind and Your Life*, conducted a study with Major League Baseball teams for two seasons, comparing their optimism and to their level of success that season. It was notable that the most optimistic team attributed their success to a one-time mistake or flaw and said room for growth was possible, demonstrating *growth mindset*.

The New York Mets displayed the most optimistic style while The St. Louis Cardinals explained their losses in a more pessimistic manner. Where an optimistic team may say, "We lost this one time, and we'll do better next time," a pessimistic team would say, "We lost because we weren't good enough, and we lack the skill to beat other teams."

Seligman and his research team predicted that the New York Mets would have a better season than the Cardinals, and in fact, for that season, that's exactly what happened.

We should also note that optimism in its extreme form can be unhealthy and do the opposite of what we want it to do in building confidence and self-worth. ***Our goal is to build a realistic optimism—meaning, looking at a situation as it truly is: the good, the bad, and the ugly. (GN#26)***

Here's a scenario that illustrates the difference between misused optimism and realistic optimism:

Scenario:
A new promotion that you would be perfect for has come about at work. You match a number of the desired qualifications and have great rapport with your current team and leader. Right before putting in your application, you find out that 16 in-house candidates have also applied for the job. Some of

applicants you know personally and can attest that they may also be a great fit for the position.

Misused Optimism: I'm qualified for the job, have worked there for a number of years, and definitely believe in myself that I can get this job over the other 16 candidates. Even though they're pretty good as well, I just know I'll get it. I believe it.

Realistic Optimism: I think I'm a great fit for the position and believe that I have a strong chance of landing the position. Although it won't be easy and there are some great candidates, I'm confident that my application will go far.

The differences between *misused* and *realistic* optimism are quite clear in that the first example completely overlooks some of the obvious challenges that relate to the situation. It is optimism with blinders on—which is never healthy. Believing in yourself is great and exactly what we want, but if we don't take into consideration the details, we can quickly lose confidence and the ability to keep trying. Our optimism slowly diminishes and our will to try goes with it.

The second example still displays a belief in oneself and the ability to succeed, but it also demonstrates a necessary understanding that it won't be easy. There's an acknowledgment of the other candidates and their qualifications. Realistic optimism recognizes it can be challenging while still achievable. They are not giving up on the belief that it will be a positive outcome, but simply looking at the big picture in its entirety.

What's important here is recognizing that when we practice realistic optimism, we build ourselves up for success and enable a mindset of growth—an attitude of "it's achievable but not necessarily easy." That last thing we want to do is build up false perceptions and exaggerated outcomes. We want the *removable* rosy-colored glasses so that we can see the fine print; and once we read the fine print, then we can put the glasses back on.

Practicing Optimism

1. *Writing Out Your Wins*

What occurred today that was a win?

_____

_____

_____

_____

What do you attribute to those wins?

_____

_____

_____

_____

2. **Careful Consumption** - *How much of what you're consuming is beneficial, uplifting, and adds value to your energy and overall success? Rate yourself on a scale of 1-10, 10 being amazing and 1 being not so good.*
   o People in your life:
   o News:
   o Food and Drinks:
   o Social Media:

Why did you give yourself the scores that you did in each category, and what is one thing you can do to increase each form of consumption?

_____

_____

_____

_____

3. ***Positive Reframing*** - Positive reframing is to perceive something previously viewed as negative in a positive light

Place a positive reframe on a difficult situation. Think of a time or situation that you currently view as negative. Is it possible to see any good in that situation or perhaps show compassion for the other party if it involved another person? What were the positives and what did you learn?

_____

_____

_____

_____

Reverse Engineering

As you work on building your C.O.R.E.², limiting beliefs and subconscious thoughts will start to show themselves and even get in your way. I encourage you to sit with these beliefs and do the reverse engineering needed to finally face the thoughts that are no longer serving you and your well-being.

Reverse engineering is an important component to building the self-love and confidence you need to get ahead in your career and life. The truth is we all have limiting beliefs, self-doubt, and fears that show up in one or more areas of our lives. You may be very strong and confident in your professional life while lacking confidence and self-love in your love life. You may feel great about your physical health and fitness and the way you look, while feeling a lack of confidence on the inside. Building your confidence and self-love goes hand-in-hand with the thoughts that show up in your brain. So how do we combat those thoughts that hold us back?

When you have negative thoughts about yourself, a feeling of doubt, or a belief that you know isn't serving you positively, I want you to stop and write it down. Then ask yourself where did these thoughts come from initially? Or, what experience in your life is associated with this thought? Keep in mind most experiences stem all the way back to our childhood or painful relationships we've had.

Here is an example from a young woman I mentored on overcoming doubt and building confidence as a public speaker:

DOUBT/FEAR: "I have a fear of public speaking and never want to do it. Even at work when I need to give presentations, I pass them on to my colleagues." (a common fear for many of us)

I REMEMBER WHEN: "I remember the last time I spoke up in front of people. I was in high school, 17 years old. After I was done presenting, the teacher laughed and told me to sit down. I felt embarrassed and not good enough."

PRACTICE:
Step 1: Write down your fear, belief, or doubt.
Step 2: Next to it, write down your past experience, which you associate with this fear or belief. (This may be the hardest part—finding the association or core of where the thought stems from.

YOUR FEAR, BELIEF, DOUBT	I REMEMBER WHEN

Step 3: Accept, Recognize, and Decide.
- Once you have identified the core of the belief, it's time to accept with compassion that you cannot rewrite the past and how it has affected you up until now. You might also be able to identify that in some cases it actually isn't your thought; it's a thought that

was put on you by perhaps your parents, your boss, and past lover.

- Recognize that your fear, belief, or doubt does not belong to you. It was put on you by a past experience, person, or even societal programming that tells you how you think you *should* be. This is their hurt, belief, and fear—not yours. Remember hurt people hurt people.

Now ask yourself: Is this belief, fear, or thought serving or hindering you? Why? The great news is you now have the ability to decide how much power you want to give this experience and/or person.

Building sustainable confidence—the key to your personal and professional success—starts within your C.O.R.E.[2] It's easy to talk about, but it is not easy. It's achievable for every person if they're willing to do the work and put forth the effort. I will tell you both from personal experience and from my experience coaching individuals around the world: the return on investment in your confidence has invaluable benefits, not only for your professional success, but for your personal success as well.

Our school systems and institutions around the world spend massive amounts of time and money developing citizens who are equipped with hard skills. But *without the confidence to take action and trust yourself, knowledge means nothing. (GN#27)* You can never reach your true potential if you don't have the confidence to take action in your personal and professional life. Whether it's your career, love life, or building connections, confidence will help you go from where you are today to where you want to be.

Emotional Intelligence

Emotional intelligence is a way of recognizing, understanding, and choosing how we think, feel, and act. It shapes our interactions with others and our understanding of ourselves. It defines how and what we learn; it allows us to set priorities; and it determines the majority of our daily actions. Research suggests it is responsible for as much as 80% of the "success" in our lives.

According to David L. Van Rooy Ph.D, Senior Director & Global Leader of Development for Walmart, and author of *Trajectory: 7 Career Strategies to Take You From Where You Are to Where You Want to Be*, "A correlation between EI and improved performance, and the validity of EI has held constant across the different performance domains, from the workplace to academic."

Emotional intelligence is broken into four quadrants: self-awareness, self-management, social awareness, and relationship management. The personal well-being of individuals and the enhancement of professional relationships are key outcomes to developing emotional intelligence.

Throughout my personal and professional experience as a trainer and coach in soft-skill competencies, I can confidently say that most challenges we see within ourselves and the workplace (whether they be small businesses or large corporations), all come down to the 18 competencies that fall under the four EI pillars.

Self Awareness	Emotional Awareness	Accurate Self Assessment	Self Confidence
Self Management	Emotion and Stress Management	Transparency	Adaptability
	Achievement	Motivation	Optimism
Social Awareness	Empathy	Service Focused	Organizational Awareness
Relationship Management	Leadership	Coaching	Relatability
	Influence	Conflict Management	Teamwork

The most successful companies and individuals are the ones who adapt their culture and communication around the key elements of EI. Workspaces and companies across the nation have now identified EI as a defining factor in company culture, productivity, and increased results. Today, companies and individuals around the world are incorporating the idea of emotional intelligence into their professional perspective and strategic outlook as well as within their personal lives.

All things start here!

One of the most important aspects of emotional intelligence is accurate self-assessment. The key to sustainable success is self-actualization. We must understand our strengths and weaknesses not only from our own perspective, but from the perspective of others. This is how we identify blind spots and whether or not our perception of ourselves is accurate.

Complete the practice below and when complete, send it to five people you trust will give you honest feedback. Have them fill it out *about you* and ask them to return the results. Now examine what you rated yourself in comparison to what they rated you. This assessment should comprise both personal and professional realms. Reminder: *work and life are not separate and are not meant to be compartmentalized. (GN#28)*

24-Point Assessment

Listed below are 24 competencies that have to do with the social and emotional intelligence. Rate yourself 1-10, 10 representing the thriving zone and 1 representing the danger zone. Add the total score of each row and divide it by 60. Write the percentage in the appropriate box below.

WITH YOURSELF

Self-Talk	Labeling Emotions	Accurate Self-Assessment	Expressing Yourself	Confidence	Realization of Triggers

Managing Emotions Stress	Intrinsic Motivation	Realistic Optimism	Resilience	Controlling Reactions	Growth Mindset

WITH OTHERS

Empathy	Active Listening	Removal of Ego	Social Awareness	Acceptance and Tolerance	Non-Verbal Cues and Posture

Leadership	Coaching/ Teaching	Solution Oriented	Relatability	Sparking Transformation	Relationship Building

Rise up for you

Human Impact. Organizational Impact. Global Impact.
www.riseupforyou.com | Rise Up For You, LLC 2020

134

"Enoughism" Turned Inwards

The final step to getting back to the core of your confidence is the most important step. Understanding "enoughism" is the last component needed to step out into life at your fullest.

Now you may be wondering what enoughism is. The term is often only heard in the consumer market in relation to product consumption and accumulation. The term was first coined by John Naish, the author of *Enough: Breaking Free From the World of More*. According to Naish, "In a world of abundance, this never-ending state of desire leads us to terrible problems." He points out that, for example, we continuously buy things that we don't have time to use. We work countless hours to buy things that merely consume space, and we complain about our well-being but we are in a constant state of material consumption that is driving our actions to produce more money and lose more time for self and others. He points out that "buying is the new worship and with shopping comes salvation. [...] If we don't learn to be content with what we have, we are destined to doom."

The true definition of enoughism states:
> A theoretical point where consumers possess everything they need, and buying more would actually make them worse off. It emphasizes less spending and more buying restraint.

Enoughism is absolutely relevant in building and regaining confidence and goes very much in hand with the underlying problem we face when it comes to self-worth. Too many of us seek outside validation from others and in stuff. Some of us buy massive amounts of shoes, purses, cars, and clothes, but for what purpose? One might be able to say it's because they have a fascination with cars or they collect vintage bags, but most of us would probably say we don't know why we are constantly buying things even when we don't need them.

Naish's concept of enoughism is clearly applicable in today's society; however, a major question in his research has yet to have really been answered: *why* do we consume so much? At the end of the day our consumption is reflective of who we are and how we feel. In fact, consumption is the key indicator of how we feel. Think about the types of food we consume, the shows and media we watch, the materialistic stuff we accumulate, and the people we allow to consume our time. The accumulated numbing effect of collecting this stuff takes us away from our core, ultimately giving us a sense of false validation—validation from people whom we feel the need to compete against or impress—validation that we are meeting the expectations of society and its so-called definition of what it means to "make it" or be successful. We are consuming things we do not need in an effort to *feel accepted*. And yet, all the while our suicide and depression rates soar across every age group in the U.S.

According to the 2019 World Happiness Report, the prevalence of addictions in the U.S. is on the rise. These addictions, in turn, cause considerable unhappiness and even depression. The implication is, therefore, that our society should begin taking actions—as individuals, in schools, at workplaces, and through public policies—to reverse this awful trend, as part of an overall strategy to increase well-being in the United States to previous levels.

The underlying problem here is that the more we consume, the more it actually worsens our ability to become awakened and truly connect with our inner self. The more we consume, the less we realize that we are enough, simply because we are! (GN#29)

I have recoined "enoughism" for the purpose of this book to say:

Individuals possess everything they need inside, and the ever-present, persistent consumption of product—whether it be media or materialistic items—makes people more disconnected and less satisfied with life. (GN#30) Enoughism emphasizes less outside validation and more inner self-development and love.

It can be challenging to sit with yourself and feel all of the hurt, past experiences, and thoughts that have made you who you are today. However, if you want to achieve internal peace and happiness, if you want to have an unstoppable confidence, you need to do the inner work without the pointless distractions around you.

Many of us seek validation externally in stuff, people, and social media. This only takes us further away from the truth that everything you need is already inside of you! Enoughism, as I recoined the term, is everywhere. This consumptive state of constantly needing, gathering, and collecting stuff is only worsening our ability to see the truth and find inner peace.

No one ever says, "Yes, I want to dig up all of my past pain and experiences." But the hard truth is that we need to go back to breaking limiting beliefs that have convinced us we are not enough. The great news is you are not alone. Every single person has some form of limiting belief that gets in their way and that plays into enoughism. Enoughism is not your fault, but the power to change it is in your hands.

No amount of materialistic items, money, or a prestigious profession can define your self-worth or your confidence. They do not make you and do not add value to your life. They are not you—**you** are you. Everything you need is already inside of you. You are enough simply because you are!

The stepping stone to your success lies with having compassion for yourself, optimism that is realistic, reverse engineering, emotional intelligence, and enoughism turned inwards. You are enough, and everything you need you already have within your *CORE!*

CHAPTER 5 GOLDEN NUGGETS

Getting back to the core of confidence and how to build confidence are stepping stones in strengthening your self-worth, rising up for you, and ultimately closing the gap in your potential.

The word self-help indicates your self is in need of help, and while that may be the case, growth doesn't need to stem from needing or wanting help. It can stem simply because you'd like to bloom into a greater version of yourself.

When we have compassion for others we are able to see that they are human, and we understand that no one is perfect.

If we can't show kindness and love to ourselves, can we really show it to others?

Our goal is to build a realistic optimism—meaning, looking at a situation as it truly is: the good, the bad, and the ugly.

Without the confidence to take action and trust yourself, knowledge means nothing.

Work and life are not separate and are not meant to be compartmentalized.

The underlying problem here is that the more we consume, the more it actually worsens our ability to become awakened and truly connect with our inner self. The more we consume, the less we realize that we are enough, simply because we are!

Individuals possess everything they need inside, and the ever-present, persistent consumption of product—whether it be media or materialistic items—makes people more disconnected and less satisfied with life.

END OF CHAPTER REFLECTIVE QUESTION:

From your perspective, being full of self-compassion and honesty, list one unhealthy thing you consume in order to make yourself feel better or to portray a certain image. For some of you, food might be the culprit that makes you feel good in times of hardship; for others, it might be purchasing clothes or *spending money* to feel important or valued in front of others. List your one go-to and ask yourself, why? Why and how does it contribute to you, and how does it make you feel? Is this a pattern you're willing to accept, or a pattern you'd like to break free of?

_____

_____

_____

_____

_____

_____

_____

Now do the reverse. What's one healthy thing you consume that makes you feel great and improves your confidence? How does it make you feel?

_____

_____

_____

CHAPTER 6
The Mainstream Mindset

CHAPTER 6

A common first question when you first meet someone is "What do you do?" Why do you think that is? As if the most important aspect of someone's identity is what they do. The worst part is people shrinking in response because they feel their job isn't valuable—maybe they aren't as successful as society tells them they ought to be. That question, "What do you do?" can sometimes portray judgment.

Personally, I have seen incredible people at Rise Up For You events, who when asked, "What do you do?" will shrink back and say something like, "Oh I'm just a mom right now." What! "Just a mom?" Do you mean the most important job on the planet (being a parent)? Do you mean the most impossible and important role there is: to empower and inspire future generations? Without present parenting, we have no lasting future! There is so much shame that circulates in this area, and unfortunately, we are managing it by working ourselves to burnout just to be able to show some sign of prestige and financial glory.

All of today's societal expectations (go to work, make money, sleep, repeat) absolutely exist. You might say this is a limiting belief of mine, but let's get real: many of us feel the repetition (the grind, the day-in day-out, the rat race) in our adult lives. And our lack of well-being proves it. It's unfortunate that we as adults feel our worth is determined by our money, job, and materialistic items.

In Europe, many professionals ride their bicycles to work. But in the US, if we saw a professional riding their bike to work, what kind of assumptions do you think we would make about them?

"They must not be able to afford a car."

"That's sad he/she has to ride their bike to work."

"I feel bad for them that they don't even have a car to get around properly."

How interesting to envision the same scenario, but in two different areas of the world with two different sets of societal norms and expectations.

Today we are in a state of moral and inner crisis. **The essence of our existence has been shrunk** *down to building a career and making money. And the hardest truth of all is that we are losing touch with our humanity and the ability to be our best in the process. (GN#31)*

Of course we have to make money, pay our bills, contribute to society through our learned professional skills, but to what end? To the point where everything else—our relationships, children, health, personal well-being, and inner fulfillment—become compromised? To what degree do we need to get to as a people to stop the enoughism, disconnectedness, and autopilot lifestyle we have created for ourselves?

So the question, again, how did we get here? Our American society often refers to itself as the world's greatest and strongest country. We are the land of the free, liberated, and lack no opportunity. With these foundational elements as part of our country, we have attracted not only a reputation that we must live up to, but an influx of international visitors and immigrants who want a crack at being abundantly successful and financially prosperous themselves.

There once was a time when immigrants coming to this country made us Americans proud. We were the envy of the world—a country where everyone wanted to live and have their chance to thrive. The name we built for ourselves in the 20th century has created a highly competitive, innovative, and diverse population. One could argue that today we continue to be a society where working hard and seeking out opportunity could allow anyone—regardless of race or gender—the opportunity to be financially and professionally successful. But with the amount of immigrants coming from abroad who do not have the same opportunities back home, the competitiveness has increased in America. More and more people are getting hungrier and hungrier for success, and they will do anything to achieve it.

Between the "American Dream" mentality, which in some ways fundamentally drives this country, and the increased competition occurring with an influx of international professionals—and then all compounded by the burgeoning world of technology—we have become a nation where working hard to be on top is the universal end-goal. Mainstream media and reality TV have set new social standards of living for many. And in the meantime our health, love lives, children, and inner-connectedness is falling apart. In an article by Eric J. Lyman, entitled "How a Belief in American Exceptionalism is Making America Less Exceptional," Lyman writes:

> I am convinced that measuring success—whether for a person, a company, or a nation—based on crude, short-term grasps for money, power, or influence, is neither sustainable nor wise.

For example, most of my friends in the U.S. think putting in hours of overtime is normal, and afterward they often continue working at home. They eat bland, unhealthy, mass-produced food packed with hormones, coloring agents, and chemical preservatives. They medicate themselves in order to sleep, and they wash down pharmaceuticals to suppress hypertension, high cholesterol, anxiety, or depression every morning with watery, over-sweetened coffee.

On average, my compatriots in the U.S. have around a third the vacation time of their European counterparts. They have less support if they lose their jobs, much less time off if they become parents, and much, much less of a voice to push for better terms within an American legal system designed to defend the rights of corporations, not individuals. Because of that, access to health care and higher education in the U.S. is increasingly seen as a luxury that will inevitably leave millions saddled in debt.

Today we are constantly seeking more money, more stuff, and more accolades, all in an effort to achieve a higher sense of worth and prestige. (GN#32) The problem lies here: everything we have learned to praise is neither consistent nor everlasting. So when the money's gone, the job has been cut, and the accolades no longer matter, who do we become?

Now is the time to recognize that we do have the power inside of us to make a shift and break the enoughism. To go against the cultural norms we have created for ourselves and build a life that we are proud of, that is fulfilling financially and professionally, and is also not dismissive of our health, community, love life, and most importantly self-worth.

When do we reach the point where enough is enough? This is a question only you can answer. Naish formulates this idea so precisely as he writes:

> The world carries on worrying about global warming, grumbling about overwork and complaining of not being happy while still chasing, making, and consuming evermore, in the hope that it will cheer everyone up. [...] We need to revive them, to evolve an 'enough' button in our culture and in our heads, to break the vicious spiral of more, more, more.

I remember this moment as if it were just yesterday: it was the day after my mother died, and I was cleaning out her closet. I am the only girl in the family so naturally all of my mother's jewelry, belongings, purses, clothes, everything was passed on to me. I remember standing there looking at all of the Louis Vuitton bags, pearl necklaces, and gold rings, thinking, wow, all this stuff is mine now! After a few minutes of cleaning and transferring the stuff to my room, I stopped dead in my tracks and just began to cry. I cried unbearably by myself. And then I started to scream.

These pearls, bags, shoes, clothes—they all meant nothing to me. None of them carried the value my mother possessed. No materialistic item or piece of jewelry could ever equal or come close to the love I was given by my mother. Now she was gone and suddenly these items didn't seem as valuable.

It was that day that a whole new sense of *what* I consume and *why* I consume it changed. I'm not only talking about materialistic items now; I'm talking about people, media, food, *things*! Enough was enough! ***I was no longer going to continue consuming things just to consume them—or to look a certain way to appease other people. (GN#33)*** Now I had the power, and it was time for me to decide what I wanted in my life and the importance behind it.

Societal pressures forcibly shape our conceptions of self-worth and identity and I knew that if I wanted to live a life I was proud of, I had to break that personal stigma within myself. I began to focus on the things in life that really mattered most, which I had ironically spent less time and money on—the things in life that we can't necessarily touch or hold, but that make us thrive and feel fulfilled when nurtured.

CHAPTER 6 GOLDEN NUGGETS

The very truth as to why we exist has been shrunk down to building a career and money. And the hardest truth to all of this is that we are losing our humanity and the ability to be our best in the process.

Today we are constantly seeking more money, more stuff, and more accolades, all in an effort to achieve a higher sense of worth and prestige.

I was no longer going to continue to consume things just to consume them or to look a certain way to appease other people.

END OF CHAPTER REFLECTIVE QUESTION:

Ask yourself the following questions with full transparency, not with shame or guilt, but transparency. There are no wrong answers here. I simply encourage you to ask yourself why behind all of the wants and needs you put on yourself.

Do you constantly feel the need to make more money? If yes, why?

_____

_____

Are you constantly buying materialistic things like clothes, bags, cars, gadgets that lie around the house? Why?

_____

_____

_____

What are your life goals in both your personal and professional life, and why? Be very specific!

PERSONAL   **PROFESSIONAL**

What type of lifestyle do you aim to have, and why?
*How much money would you **realistically** need a*
month to make that happen?

_____

_____

_____

Again there are no wrong answers! I would be
untruthful if I said I didn't like nice shoes and pretty
dresses. The point here is to simply ask yourself
why? Only you can have an honest conversation
with yourself and answer these questions.

After doing this exercise what have you discovered
about yourself?

_____

_____

_____

_____

CHAPTER 7
Becoming Your Best -
The 6 Pillars to Success

CHAPTER 7

I'm sitting here in a small cafe in Nyhavn, Denmark, one of the charming cities of greater Copenhagen, eating a fresh croissant, drinking coffee, and enjoying the people as they stroll by in the rain. May 21, 2019, marks the first day of my Scandinavian adventure where I walk the streets alone, observe their way of life, and attempt to spark conversations with strangers as a way to stay connected. You may be thinking: why Scandinavia? And what does that have to do with this book? Over the past five years, the Scandinavian countries Denmark, Sweden, and Norway have topped the charts as the happiest people in the world, according to the World Happiness Report.

In becoming your best self, it's important to know that culture and community play a part in how we define "becoming your best." What do these countries practice that, year after year, they find themselves among the happiest people in the world? And why has the U.S. fallen on this chart for the third year in a row? According to Jon Magnussen, a professor of Health Economics at the Norwegian University of Science and Technology and the University of Oslo, he says:

> The Scandinavian model of the welfare state has become internationally known. It is characterized by the state playing a dominant role in the formation of welfare policies and a corresponding extensive public sector for the implementation of these policies. Although there are many country-specific attributes, similar features include a broad scope of social policies, universal social benefits, and free or heavily subsidized services.

One of the notable differences in well-being in Scandinavian countries is that the basic necessities that contribute to a thriving life are already taken care of for their citizens, creating less overall stress. For example, universal healthcare is provided for all citizens regardless of race, income, or social class.

When my father passed away from a heart attack, he did not have insurance as a self-employed business man. After his death, my family and I received a stream of medical bills in the mail for hundreds of thousands of dollars. Looking at the bills was overwhelming and scary! The ambulance ride alone was billed at $33,000 dollars for a two-mile ride. How the heck were three young adults in their twenties going to pay hundreds of thousands of dollars? The stress of it was crippling.

The *Health Management Journal* states:

> The Nordic healthcare system has a long heritage. It is especially well-established with regard to primary and preventive healthcare. These couple into sophisticated occupational health standards which are considered to be models by the outside world. All Nordic countries also have highly-developed hospital services. Nordic healthcare systems are taxation based, and locally administrated with every citizen having equal access to services [...] At a political level, equity and equality are important priorities.

In addition, Magnussen further explains:

> Scandinavian healthcare systems are built on the same principles of universalism, strongly expressing a goal of equal access to services regardless of social class, income, or place of residence. To reach this goal, the Scandinavian model has relied on public ownership and control, limited use of market-based incentives such as choice or

competition, and rationing in the form of (at times long) waiting lists.

Another major difference is the Scandinavian education system in comparison to the American counterpart. A recent 2019 study showed that "Americans owe over $1.56 trillion in student loan debt, spread out among about 45 million borrowers. That's about $521 billion more than the total U.S. credit card debt."

In another article published in *Forbes*, "Student Loan Debt Statistics In 2019: A $1.5 Trillion Crisis" the author states, "Student loan debt is now the second highest consumer debt category—behind only mortgage debt—and higher than both credit cards and auto loans."

The effects of student loan debt have delivered a huge blow to the well-being of American college graduates and students. Executive Director of Student Debt Crisis, Natalia Abrams says, "We do get stories of borrowers who are struggling with the idea of suicide," and that student debt has created "a disastrous domino effect for millions of Americans."

In Nordic countries, we see that education is not only highly valued by their governments but provided free for their citizens and even to some international students. In a recent article, "Why Study at

Scandinavian Universities?" the financial benefits are clearly drawn out.

In Denmark, tuition remains free for all EU/EEA students and students on exchange programs. In Sweden, there are no fees for citizens of EU/EEA countries, Ph.D students, or programs taught in Swedish.

Public universities in Norway are still free for students of all nationalities, at all study levels. There's just a very small fee of NOK300-600 (~US$37-74) per semester. Private universities in Norway do charge fees, but they are relatively low, and are the same for both local and international students.

Lastly, a major difference and contributor in well-being is the public policy around parenting and having children.

In some ways, these countries offer their citizens an advantage toward becoming their best selves as the basics of healthcare, education, and family time are covered and actively promoted by its country's leaders. It can feel like a never-ending cycle to work all day to gain healthcare benefits, to pay off student debt, to eventually live a free life while in the meantime you're stressed about family time, playing with your kids, and trying to take care of your own health. For many, by the time they feel a sense of freedom, they have already mismanaged their health, missed out on parenting opportunities, and/or are potentially moving toward a divorce or going through multiple heartbreaks due to ignoring their relationships.

This is not a cry out to point fingers and say we are doomed. On the contrary, this is to say that we must take our power back and build the best life we can because no one else is going to do it or even foster a space for it. You must recognize that **every decision you make should move you towards this driving initiative:** *what does it mean to build a life you are proud of—to become your best self? (GN#34)* At the end of the day, what would give you the ability to say, "If my last day on earth were tomorrow, I would be okay because I lived the best life I could live on my own terms."

One challenge to this question is rewriting what it means to be professionally and personally successful. You've probably heard you should be: married with kids before 30, buying your first home before 40, no student loan debt from school, an executive title in the workforce, making six figures, etc. I'll be honest and say I fell into this trap! I was too concerned with checking off the little boxes of what I thought I *should* be to everyone else that I forgot about who I wanted and needed to be for me.

Is this success? And if it is, what happens if the market crashes again like it did in 2008? Your home forecloses, you lose your job, you start accumulating more debt because of it. Or more relatable to today, what happens when a pandemic hits and uncertainty sweeps across the world? Are you then no longer successful? Did you somehow actually fail at life? Or do you still have something to live for?

Your time is now to create your success and get to the next level which is in alignment with your life and heart. For some, this may mean living a humble life in a one-bedroom apartment and saving money to travel the world. For others, it means doing yoga every day and connecting with the self and building new connections with diverse people. What does it mean for you?

PRACTICE: I will refer back to Chapter 3 and now ask you:

"What does it mean to live a life that I am proud of?"
"What does it look like? "
"Are you there now, almost there, or far behind?

Through extensive research and personal experience, coaching various organizations and individuals, Rise Up For You has defined The Six Pillars of Life as the blueprint for building your best life and becoming your best self.

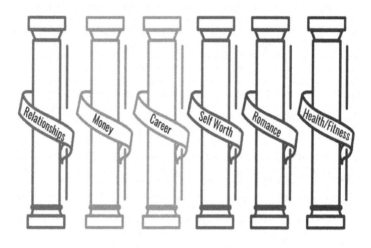

= Becoming Your Best Self

© Rise Up For You, LLC, 2020

When we examine the elements that affect us and our well-being the most, we can break it down to these six areas:

Relationships

This pillar's specific focus is on communication, leadership skills, and soft skills—such as emotional and social intelligence, conflict resolution, and networking strategies. This does not include your romantic life as we have classified that as a separate pillar.

Individuals are affected and influenced by those who surround them. Building professional and personal relationships is a crucial part of your happiness and success. *Anything great that has ever been achieved usually comes from a collection of minds and a community of support. (GN#35)*

You may be familiar with the famous quote from Jim Rohn: "You are the average of the five people you spend the most time with." Shilagh Mirgain, Ph.D UW Health Psychologist echoes this famous sentiment as she explains that "happiness isn't just a personal experience, it is actually affected by the individuals around you." Mirgain continues:

> How an individual feels can ripple through his or her social groups and actually influence how the group feels in general [...] In some ways, our emotional states are like a virus— we can spread the positive and negative experience to those around us, even with strangers.

Research from Mirgain also suggests that the effects of a positive relationship are four to seven times greater than the impact of a negative relationship. Mirgain, along with many others, suggest that creating physical and emotional distance is a key indicator in staying positive and limiting your level of impact.

Money

In modern society, money rules all. In spite of its undeniable utility, money is also one of the top stressors for Americans and exercises a unique power over us, which has ultimately led to millions of divorces, unhealthy work habits, and low estimations of self-worth.

According to a new survey by Ramsey Solutions, "money fights are the second-leading cause of divorce, behind infidelity. Results show that both high levels of debt and a lack of communication are major causes for the stress and anxiety surrounding household finances."

Understanding how to make money work for you is crucial in formulating a financial plan. This pillar is specific to financial literacy, money management, budgeting, investing, and spending habits and beliefs.

The biggest question to ask yourself regarding this category is: what do you want, and why? Formulating an arbitrary goal because you think having *this thing* equals success is not sustainable. Ask yourself what you *really* want in regards to money without allowing outside/societal forces to influence your thoughts.

Career

In 2019, 3.5 million Americans quit their jobs every single month. 50% of the American workforce are disengaged at work just getting by, and a whopping 20% are completely miserable. Only 30% of the workforce in America actually enjoy what they do in a corporate environment. This has been one of the key factors for the rise in coaches, consultants, and small online start-ups. People today want more than a paycheck. *The modern day workforce wants meaning, growth, development, positive leadership, and most importantly, a trajectory for their career laid out. (GN#36)*

People are hungry to make an impact and are seeking something more in life. Today our careers have become an outlet mostly because we either choose or are required to dedicate the majority of your days focused on work.

The main question here is: what do you want in your career, why do you want it, and what is it going to take to get there if you're not there already?

Self-Worth

If you remember anything from this book, remember this: *self-actualization and self-worth are the key to sustainable success.* Your potential and your ability to grow and build a life that you are proud of is fully dependent on how you feel and what you think about yourself. Your thoughts and beliefs about yourself drive your actions, motivations, and the ability to make decisions which are in alignment with your true authentic self.

Too many of us are searching outside of ourselves, and in return we make choices that ultimately don't fully serve us or our desired destination. (GN#37)

I'm a firm believer that everything we experience is meant to teach us a lesson. But at what point do we self-actualize and recognize that everything we need is already inside of us? We have to go back to our ancestors' ways of relying on our own power and putting our voice and intuition before others.

Humanity today is in a state of crisis where we no longer have trust in ourselves. There is so much noise around us that has created a disconnectedness with the earth, others, and most importantly within ourselves. In order to build a life we are proud of and truly tap into our fullest potential, we must start here before all other pillars.

Romance

The truth is everyone loves and needs to be loved. Romantic partners fulfill a different need in you and your psyche than any other person in your life, which is why this pillar is separate from the Relationship Intelligence pillar.

Unfortunately, work, life, and our own insecurities tend to put our romantic relationships at risk of survival or even existence at all. We all want love, but we choose work and answering our cell phone at dinner over a romantic date night instead. We want to settle down, but first there is a huge checklist of expectations that must be met. We complain that the connection is dying, but work, friends, our egos, and external factors take priority over our partners.

This pillar matters because it affects us mentally, physically, and emotionally, on a level that is inexplicable. Nights where you can't sleep because you got into an argument, the deep pit in your stomach when you have a break-up, yet you still need to show up at work with your best foot forward. Lonely nights that make you question if you're really worthy of someone else's love. We've all been there and we've all felt the effects.

The romance pillar ties directly into self-worth and confidence. The more value and love we have for ourselves, the more inclined we are to make the right decisions when it comes to picking the right partner and being in a committed relationship. Furthermore, the more we develop our relationship intelligence, the more we understand why we and our partners behave the way we do.

What do you want in a partner and what are the non-negotiables? Ask yourself and those close to you who have a strong relationship if your non-negotiables are realistic or filled with expectations that go beyond our control. *We often mix up values and the foundation of love for self-serving expectations that we project onto our partners. (GN #38)* Your partner doesn't need to be your lover, best friend, therapist, workout buddy, personal chef, movie companion, career coach, etc. They don't need to pick up a fork and eat like you, wash their hands in the exact same fashion, and have the exact same hobbies. Figure out what really matters and focus on those non-negotiables that you truly need and want in your partner. From here on out, you can be clear on what does not align with you and your heart.

Health and Fitness

Does it make sense to you that we spend our whole life building our wealth to then turn it around and spend it on our health? We fall into this trap of external praise and materialistic glory and forget how important it is to nurture our physical, nutritional, and mental health. YES! All three of them matter. This is not about weight, looks, or the ability to rock a bikini body. This is about longevity, mobility, and the ability to function at your best ability in life, at work, for your family, and for yourself.

Today we have the highest suicide and depression rates while the cases of cardiac disease and cancer continue to decline, and more and more people are losing their health and ability to enjoy life in their body because of causes that are *"yet to be determined."* **In this competitive, fast-paced world full of grab-and-go eating and the hustle-grind mentality, we are slowly losing our sanity, mobility, and connectedness to food and its real purpose for the human body. (GN#39)**

How many times have you said, "You're going to start today!" "Today, my health matters."

My father was 30 when he had his first heart attack, and when he was 63, he died from the sixth one. He wasn't overweight, he wasn't immobile, but he was stressed and on the go to build a better life for himself and his family.

Don't wait until it's too late.

The Six Pillars to Success Exercise - Part 1

Let's take a moment and assess where you are in each pillar of life currently. Follow the Six Pillars to Success self-assessment and let's begin the journey to become your best. *But...* before we start, this exercise must be done with self-compassion (the first step to C.O.R.E^2) This isn't about perfection! This is about having an honest conversation about where you are now and where you want and deserve to be.

Rate each pillar 1-10 according to the following scale:

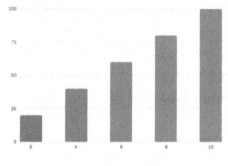

1-2= Needs a lot of work and is far from my goal. I am not happy with this at all!

3-4= It's existent but not consistent. I'm not happy with this.

5-6= Needs improvement but I am half way there. More hard work and I'll achieve my level of happiness in this pillar.

7-8= I am happy with this pillar! I'm really close to exactly what I want and I feel pretty great about it.

9-10= I feel great! This pillar is in alignment with me and I feel that I am currently at my best!

This is a great visual indicator to address which areas need more love and nurturing. Rate each pillar 1-10, 10 being your optimal thriving zone and 1 being your danger zone. How off balance is your circle? For your lowest pillar, what is one thing you can do to get to your next level in the next month?

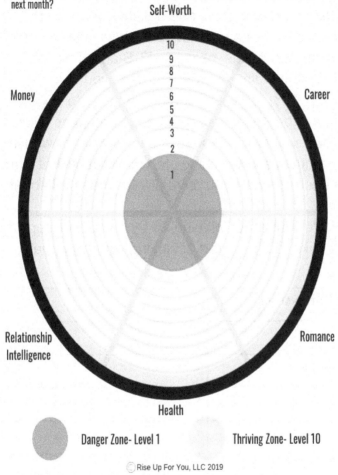

Danger Zone- Level 1   Thriving Zone- Level 10

The 6 Pillars to Success Exercise - Part 2

Now that you have evaluated each element, let's develop specific goals and outline a plan to achieve them. What small, actionable steps can you take now to rise to the next level? Start small, so you don't overwhelm yourself. Perhaps you can start by saving 10% of your monthly income to invest in future property, working out for 10 minutes twice a week if you haven't exercised in a while, or working 30 minutes every night to start formulating that start-up business idea you have always dreamed about!

Create your action plan below by listing one step you can take today to start achieving your new goals.

RELATIONSHIPS	1.
MONEY	1.
CAREER	1.
SELF-WORTH	1.
ROMANCE	1.
HEALTH AND FITNESS	1.

The beautiful thing about this assessment is that it's never too late to start working towards your level 10 in all six pillars. Remember life is always changing, so revisit this exercise every three months and watch your levels of happiness increase as you

transform into becoming your best self.
It won't come overnight (and it won't be easy), but just remember you are capable and have the power to step into this life at 1000%. The power is all yours!

CHAPTER 7 GOLDEN NUGGETS

Every decision you make should move you towards this driving initiative: what does it mean to build a life you are proud of—to become your best self?

Anything great that has ever been achieved usually comes from a collection of minds and a community of support.

The modern day workforce wants meaning, growth, development, positive leadership, and most importantly, a trajectory for their career laid out.

Too many of us are searching outside of ourselves, and in return we make choices that ultimately don't fully serve us or our desired destination.

We often mix up values and the foundation of love for self-serving expectations that we project onto our partners.

In this competitive, fast-paced world full of grab-and-go eating and the hustle-grind mentality, we are slowly losing our sanity, mobility, and connectedness to food and its real purpose for the human body.

END OF CHAPTER REFLECTIVE QUESTION:

How did the 6 Pillars to Success Exercise make you feel? Did you have any new revelations of epiphanies about where you are today and where you want to go?

_____

_____

_____

_____

_____

_____

CHAPTER 8
Closing Your Potential Gap

CHAPTER 8

"Try it again, and this time go for the note in full voice. Belt that sucker out," I said.

"I can't," said Jessica, the room in motion behind her, full of 150 other singers and dancers.

"Yes, you can! Trust me, I can hear it in your voice. You will not crack. You can sing another five notes above where you're stopping in a full belt. Don't think, don't get in your head, just do it!"

Suddenly, she was out there on stage, singing, "Like a bridge over troubled water, I *way* lay me down, Like a bridge over troubled water.... I *will* lay me down."

The room went wild, it was the first time Jessica had belted a note that high. She had even shocked herself. As she came off stage looking at me, she said, "Oh my gosh, I've never sung that high. I'm shaking."

"I know. You have to believe in yourself. You have to push yourself even if you're not sure you will make it. It's the only way you will grow your voice."

Today one of the most common challenges I see among people—young kids, working professionals, it's not limited to any one age group—is the lack of ability to push themselves and to tap into their full (or even half) their potential.

The truth is we all have blind spots, meaning we don't know what we don't know. (GN #40) Often it can be tough to push ourselves because we're not even sure of our own capabilities. For many, failure is not an option to entertain.

Closing the gap between you and your potential is the only way you can truly become your best, and yet very few of us wake up every morning with the intention and drive to give everything we got. Yes! Becoming friendly with failure and falling is a part of closing your potential gap. When we shy away from failure, when we're scared to make mistakes, or in the case of Jessica, afraid your voice might crack, you stop yourself from ever reaching the next level of growth, that potential which is just waiting to burst out of you.

Let's suppose I asked you the following. On a scale of 1-10, how would you rate yourself? 10 being "yes, all the way" and 1 being "barely—not even existent."

1. Are you using your full potential at work? 1-10: _____
2. Are you using your full potential when it comes to your health? 1-10: _____
3. Are you using your full potential in your romantic life? 1-10: _____
4. Are you using your full potential in life in general? 1-10: _____

What did you give yourself and why? The big question, why aren't you using your full potential and what's stopping you?

_____

_____

_____

_____

So, you've had the chance to understand your Six Pillars; you know what success looks like for you. But most importantly, we need to find out how to close the potential gap and actually make progress towards becoming a better version of ourselves. It's great to do these exercises, but let's remind ourselves: **Without strategic action steps and a committed intent to be better, any sort of activity, reflective questioning, or goal-setting you could do will simply remain some "fairytale" idea, never to be fulfilled. You need a plan and the commitment to see your plan through (GN #41)** Only 30% of individuals accomplish their new-year goals, which directly proves my point.

So! How do we actually go about closing the potential gap, and where do we start?

There are five crucial steps to supporting your potential and greatness. Each one of these steps must be very intentional in it's practice and may take some time to cultivate.

How do we close the potential gap?

STEP #1 - Confidence

Chapters 4 and 5 are heavily focused on confidence, so I'll keep this first step short and only remind you of how important it is.

According to our research surveying a group of over 1,000 working professionals, 80% of them reported struggling with confidence. When asked, "What is your top challenge today as a working professional?" here are some of their responses:
- "I don't feel like I am enough."

- "I'm constantly doubting myself and my abilities, and I know it's holding me back."
- "I'm not as good as I should be at work, and I don't know why."
- "I don't know how to advocate and stick up for myself. I watch other people get opportunities and I just stand there passively wishing for more."
- "I have great ideas that I would love to share, but I don't speak up for fear of sounding stupid or inadequate."
- "I feel stuck and every day my confidence shrinks because I'm not doing anything about it."
- "I feel that I need to be perfect so I'm not taking any risks."

Do any of these sound like you? 80% is a huge number of people who don't feel confident and who in turn are not using their potential. It's sad honestly, and it hasn't changed. More recently, we did our traditional survey with a new corporate client and we saw a similar result. Not feeling good enough and not having the confidence to take action and live the life we are destined to live is a tragedy that must be avoided. I'll say it again and again, *"The greatest tragedy today is wasted human potential." (GN #42)*

STEP #2 - Consumption Management

Do you ever wake up in the morning feeling completely drained and exhausted but not sure why? You just slept for hours and you're still waking up as if you've had no sleep? How about going through your day and by 2:00 you're completely fried mentally. You have nothing to give, nothing to say, and all you can think about is, "Why am I so tired!"

I think many of us can agree, that especially in 2020, this sounds like us more often than not! My friends, welcome to the effects of consumption overload!

According to a number of recent surveys, The average American spends 5.4 hours a day on their phone with 144 minutes per day spent on social media.

According to J. Clement with Statista:

> Social media has a wide-reaching and significant impact on not only online activities but also offline behavior and life in general. During a global online user survey in February 2019, a significant share of respondents stated that social media had increased their access to information, ease of communication, and freedom of expression. On the flipside, respondents also felt that social media had worsened their personal

privacy, increased a polarization in politics and heightened everyday distractions.

In addition, the *LA Times* recently published an article featuring the staggering statistics about the collective surge in watching and consuming news.

> Fox News had its most-watched week of 2020 from March 16 to March 22, with an average of 2.5 million throughout the day, a 73% increase over a comparable week last year. It was followed by CNN's 1.55 million viewers, which was up 151% from last year, and MSNBC, which drew 1.48 million viewers for a 45% gain.

> The three broadcast network evening newscasts, which have seen their clout diminish in recent years as more viewers turn to cable and the internet, are seeing their highest viewing levels in more than 15 years. Last week, they averaged 32 million viewers, according to Nielsen. That was the most viewers since January 2004, before streaming and the widespread use of DVRs.

Now to be fair, we can assume that these numbers are a direct result of COVID-19 and working remotely; however, it does not take away from the fact that we are consuming more and more each day which directly affects our mental stimuli, the ability to focus, and our overall stress levels.

According to the *Harvard Business Review*,

> ...the surging volume of available information—and its interruption of people's work—can adversely affect not only personal well-being but also decision making, innovation, and productivity. In one study, for example, people took an average of nearly 25 minutes to return to a work task after an e-mail interruption. That's bad news for both individuals and their organizations.

> Researchers say that the stress of not being able to process information as fast as it arrives—combined with the personal and social expectation that, say, you will answer every email message—can deplete and demoralize you. Edward Hallowell, a psychiatrist and expert on attention-deficit disorders, argues that the modern workplace induces what he calls "attention deficit trait," with characteristics similar to those of the genetically based disorder. Author Linda Stone, who coined the term "continuous partial attention" to describe the mental state of today's knowledge workers, says she's now noticing—get this—"e-mail apnea": the unconscious suspension of regular and

steady breathing when people tackle their e-mail.

There are even claims that the relentless cascade of information lowers people's intelligence. A few years ago, a study commissioned by Hewlett-Packard reported that the IQ scores of knowledge workers distracted by email and phone calls fell from their normal level by an average of 10 points—twice the decline recorded for those smoking marijuana, several commentators wryly noted.

All of this to say, we are heavily impacted by all of the things we consume on a daily basis. The consumption is overwhelming, more than what we need, and often addicting. Here is what I like to call the Fuzzy Four, because with too much consumption that's exactly what happens; we become fuzzy, drained, and unable to even begin closing our potential gap.

1. **People** - Everyone carries a different energy, attitude and beliefs with them and they directly affect how we connect and interact with one another. Consuming energies of other people may not always be a great thing especially if they take away from your energy,

put you down, or leave you feeling drained on multiple occasions.

2. **Food and Drinks** - What type of food and drinks are you consuming on a daily basis? Overall, is your nutritional lifestyle healthy and energy-boosting or is it filled with foods that are high in chemical content, which affect your levels of energy and physical mobility? Everything we consume in our body will directly affect our mind and physical capabilities.

3. **Social Media** - Our society's over-reliance on our cell phones and the convenient apps they feature is obvious to everyone. I know I'm guilty of waking up in the morning and reaching for my phone first, sometimes even before I acknowledge my loved ones and say good morning to them. But think about it, I bring in *thousands* of people into my consciousness every morning through social media and the news. And sometimes I'm completely drained by them before the sun has even fully risen because I've already brought in a bevy of mundane, pointless information and selfies of random people. Are you getting stuck in the media madness—going mad and losing valuable brain power and energy to stories, pictures, and fake news on social media that rarely contribute to your mental stimulation?

4. **Watch and Hear** - Similar to social media, what we see and hear directly affects our mental awareness and productivity. In addition, the type of shows and music we consume also make an impact on our energy and stress levels. For example, in an article from *US News and World Report*, "The relationship between violent media use and aggression and desensitization to violence is as strong as or stronger than the relationship between smoking and lung cancer," says David L. Hill, author of *Dad to Dad: Parenting Like A Pro*. Research shows that early exposure to TV violence also makes it likelier that kids will grow up to be aggressive adults."

Consumption overload is a real thing and it takes away from the productivity, focus, and energy you will need to close your potential gap and be your best. (GN#43)

On a scale of 1-10, rate yourself on the **Fuzzy Four**. 10—meaning your consumption is low, 1—meaning you consume way too much.

Fuzzy Four	Reflective Question	Rate yourself 1-10
People	Overall, how do you feel about the people who are currently most often around you?	
Food and Drinks	What does your daily food and intake look like? What types of food?	
Social Media	Average consumption time each day?	
Watch and Hear	Average consumption time each day?	

STEP #3 - Meaning, Not Purpose

Pardon me, but I have a bone to pick with purpose! The amount of times I've heard influencers and other people—including myself—say, "Find your purpose," it's deafening. And today, **purpose** is still splashed all over social media and firmly in place in the motivational world's vernacular. Phrases like, "Find your *purpose*," "What *is* your *purpose*?" "Pursue your *purpose*."

The truth is closing your potential gap and becoming your best has very little to do with purpose. Every single person has purpose in what they do and it's important for us to reframe what *purpose* is.

Unfortunately, the word has become something it's not. It's becoming an all too common sight to see people quitting their jobs, feeling inadequate, and struggling to find value in life because they don't know what their purpose is—or because they don't feel they're living with purpose.

Let's be clear on what the true definition of purpose is: *the reason for which something is done or created or for which something exists.*

I've had parents sit in front of me with multiple children and say they don't have purpose. I've had professionals who run million-dollar companies with hundreds of employees say they don't have purpose. I've had students who are getting a top-quality education for a brighter, better prepared future say they don't have purpose.

Every single one of these individuals has purpose. Purpose is not the problem! The question is whether or not an individual finds meaning in what they are doing, in the life they are leading. (GN#44)

Now, the word *meaning* on the other hand...

Meaning: *important or worthwhile quality, implied or explicit significance*

This is the question! Do you currently feel that your work, your personal life, relationships, all have meaning? You may not find purpose in building a spreadsheet for work, but one could argue that your particular function is *quite* important from a CEO's or organizational management perspective. So, if you don't find meaning in building a spreadsheet, well then it's clear that the importance of that task, role, or job is not something that you care enough about to pursue. In other words, are you able to assign meaning to your job function in order to create a sense of purpose? If not, then maybe a change is needed.

What brings you meaning in work?

_____

_____

What does it mean to you to have meaningful relationships?

_____

_____

STEP #4 - Pursued Development

Closing the potential gap does not happen overnight. It takes hard work and a growth mindset each and every day. It's easy to start something, but it's much more difficult to stick with it and see it through to completion.

If you want to close the potential gap, if you want to be your best, then you must constantly put yourself out there to pursue growth and opportunities. This is the difference between *wishing* you had more of something and *taking action* in order to make it happen.

The more we grow ourselves and learn new skills, meet new people, and try new things, the more we have an understanding of our strengths and weaknesses, we uncover our blind spots, and we begin to trust more in our current abilities *and* untapped, *potential* abilities.

If you're unsure how to pursue growth, here are some examples:

- Attend conferences, networking events, and seminars to learn new skills and gain self-empowerment
- Take courses at a local or online college on topics that interest you or potential career fields
- Hire a coach to help you improve in areas where you need improvement, support, accountability, strategy, and clarity
- Make it a point to try new things (at least) every month—familiarize yourself with being uncomfortable and remain a learner
- Travel with the intention of trying new things, new foods, and learning about new cultures

- Listen to interesting podcasts or watch inspiring or helpful videos (like TEDx talks) that can aid to your development
- Have open conversations with people who have a different perspective or culture than you. Question your own thought processes and try to learn more about others' ways of thinking. The key here is to be open, not to spark confrontation and/or descend into emotional arguments.
- Every week take small steps to push yourself outside your normal comfort zone. Try writing with the opposite hand, wearing an outfit you normally wouldn't pick, or taking a dance class for fun without expectations!

All too often our own personal and professional growth is put on the back burner. I always hear people say, "I don't have time," or "I'm too busy." Well, we can't have our cake and eat it too! If you want the job promotion, if you want to see more clients calling for your services, if you want to get to your next level, then you must put energy, time, and commitment into growing yourself. No more excuses, no more hesitation, just do it. If you're not ready to invest your time, energy, and even money in developing yourself, then you're not ready to become your best. Something or someone has taken priority over your growth and your life and that needs to change first.

Fill out this statement:

Today, my personal and professional development is _____ priority (be truthful— *top*, *bottom*, *somewhat of a* priority).

I have chosen to put _____ over my own growth, and I would like to change that, starting today. So, I will _____ every _____ (how often) to begin my journey toward closing my potential gap.

STEP #5 - Community & Your Personal Board

Jim Rohn said it beautifully, "You are the average of the five people you spend the most time with." Whether or not we want to admit it, people affect us in both positive and, well, sometimes not-so-positive ways. Regardless of their contribution, you must recognize that we all need other people to build our own personal successes. *Nothing great can be done alone. It takes a community of loving and supportive people along the way to help us close our potential gap. (GN#45)*

I am a firm believer that every single person should have their own personal Board of Directors! Yes, you're very own Board made up of five unique people who can support your journey and help you get to your next step in life personally and professionally.

1. **The Cheerleader** pours affirmations and love on to you especially when you're feeling down and discouraged. They don't provide feedback or give you advice, they simply remind you of how amazing you are, cheer you up, and offer positive affirmations to you to encourage your forward movement.

2. **The Mentor** guides and teaches you, using their own personal experiences, so your path can be made that much easier. The Mentor has walked in your future footsteps, so they are well versed in where you want to be or what you want to do. If you were trying to build a business, for example, the Mentor might be the successful, self-made business owner who lends you trusted advice and guidance.

3. **The Constructive Trustee** holds you accountable and tells you like it is! They keep you in check when you go off track, and they point out your personal blind spots. The key here is to ensure your Constructive Trustee provides *constructive* feedback that you are ready to receive openly. If their feedback or demeanor is too harsh, you may shut down. If they are not direct enough, their feedback may go over your head. It's important to find

the right type of personality and person for this to ensure you're truly benefiting.

4. **The Connector** keeps you top-of-mind in their circle of friends and when they are networking. If you're looking for a romantic partner, the Connector thinks of you when they meet another single person who might be a good fit. If you're looking for more business for your technology company, they're thinking of you when they hear people mention challenges and struggles when it comes to technology in their business. They connect you with the right people to leverage your personal and/or professional success.

5. **The Advocate** is a high-stakes individual who sticks their neck out for your growth or success. This is the individual who helps you get the promotion, the person that constantly talks you up to other executives to help you get seen, the person that drives business your way because they believe so much in you that they're willing to stake their name on it!

Your personal Board of Directors is a must-have and essential to supporting your growth and closing the gap in your potential. As you build your Board, a few more things to think about in the process:

1. They may already exist in your network. Check your phone; look at your LinkedIn

community. Whom do you already know that can fill these roles?

2. Add value! Don't expect your small group of your closest friends to suddenly become your personal Board overnight and start serving you. You must serve first, always, and cultivate a relationship of trust, loyalty, and support first.

3. If you don't have someone that can fill a board position, go find them! Network, connect with new people, and start to fill up your personal community with people you admire and respect. Think about where they network, what type of events do they go to, and how they serve the community.

Closing your potential gap is possible, and everything you need to do so is right here in this book, in these chapters. The only thing that is going to stop you now is you! Do not let that happen. Start creating a plan for yourself and start taking action.

CHAPTER 8 GOLDEN NUGGETS

The truth is we all have blind spots, meaning we don't know what we don't know.

Without strategic action steps and a committed intent to be better, any sort of activity, reflective questioning, or goal-setting you could do will simply remain some "fairytale" idea, never to be fulfilled. You need a plan and the commitment to see your plan through.

The greatest tragedy today is wasted human potential.

Consumption overload is a real thing and it does take away from the productivity, focus, and energy you need each and every day to close your potential gap and be your best.

Every single one of these individuals has purpose. Purpose is not the problem! The question is whether or not an individual finds meaning in what they are doing and within the life they are leading.

Nothing great can be done alone. It takes a community of loving and supportive people along the way to help us close our potential gap.

END OF CHAPTER REFLECTIVE EXERCISE:

Let's start building your board! Who do you know that can potentially serve on your personal board of directors?

CHEERLEADER:_____

MENTOR: _____

CONSTRUCTIVE TRUSTEE: _____

CONNECTOR: _____

ADVOCATE: _____

CONCLUSION
It's Up To You Now

CHAPTER 9

I began this book by sharing my story and journey with you, not because I needed to but because I wanted you to understand that every single person is subject to the sometimes wanton ebbs and flows of life. Life does not discriminate against any one single person. We all suffer hurt, trauma, heartbreak, death. We've all been put down, told we can't do something—the list goes on. These experiences in life directly affect how we show up at work, how we lead, parent, and how we show up in the world.

We always have choices in our lives. To be or not to be! You will either rise up for you and be your best regardless of what comes your way, or you will allow things and people who do not serve you and your vision to keep you cemented in the past. Which will you choose?

Do not let these experiences allow you to play small or to stop yourself from achieving and becoming the person you want to be.

As I mentioned before, it's not easy. There may be someone you need to forgive, something you need to overcome, or beliefs you need to break in order to move forward. Whatever it is—start. Figure it out today, and start walking forward. Even if it's not a straight road—which, I can tell you, it won't be— keep moving forward. Keep taking steps toward closing your potential gap and becoming your best.

Our households, workspaces, communities, and most importantly, the next generation all depend on us to show them how to lead confidently and lovingly in this world. If we can't cultivate greatness within ourselves, if we can't close our potential gaps, how can we expect to pass it down to others? How can we expect others to treat us with greatness, and see the potential in us?

This book was designed to take you through the three phases of tapping into your potential:

- Building Confidence and Self-Worth to take Action
- Redefining Success as the Whole Person to Understand What You Want
- Create a plan to close the potential gap through building confidence, limiting

unnecessary consumption, find meaning, developing yourself constantly, and creating your personal Board of Directors.

Remember, it doesn't matter how many degrees or certifications you have, or how much money you make, if you don't have the confidence to take action, clarity to know where you are going, and the strategy to implement your goals, nothing will serve you the way you deserve to be served.

I've said it multiple times, and I'll end the book by saying it again:

The greatest tragedy is wasted human potential. Do not let that be your story!

ACKNOWLEDGEMENTS

My life and this book would not be what it is today if it weren't for a number of amazing people who have modeled greatness, passion, and kindness throughout my upbringing and young adult life.

First and foremost, I am forever grateful for my parents Nabih Salman Nasserdeen and Adele Kanso. Although they left this world too soon, they were quality parents who loved my brothers and me unconditionally. They never allowed us to play small, put ourselves down, question God, or be unkind to anyone! They loved deeply and although our time together was short, the quality of love is worth a million lifetimes.

To my brothers Walid Nasserdeen and Jamal Nasserdeen. Thank you for always pushing me and keeping me accountable when I get off track. You both have been my rock since we were kids, and our love for one another is a reflection of our parents. I hope one day you will also write your magnificent story as two resilient men who have touched the lives of many people.

To my grandma Bahia Kansao: your confidence, wisdom, and respect for yourself has provided an unshakeable strength, wisdom, and groundedness in my soul.

To my continued Merhi family, Umo Sami, Aunt Camelia, Maheba, Raja, Fadia, Rema, and Rami. We're in this together, side by side. Our families have and always will be a singular unit. Your love and open house has never gone unnoticed.

I love you all.

To the many other changemakers in my life around the world who have led the way and inspired me beyond words.

Bill and Robyn Brawley for your unwavering support and mentorship to people around the world for over 50 years. I look forward to seeing your book on my nightstand.

Sano in Japan and Nartan Hieb in Germany for your dedication and passion to change the world and inspire today's youth.

To the resilient and passion driven Rise Up For You Team for standing by my side and the mission to serve humanity. Special shout out to our editor Seth Johansson for reading every line of this book in an effort to positively transform the readers.

And lastly to you the reader for showing up. Showing up is the hardest thing to do and starting with this book is a clear sign that you are ready. You are ready to Rise Up For You and awaken the infinite potential within. The world is waiting for you.

The Family- Mom and Dad

Sibling Love   **Mom and Me**

The places I've traveled while writing the book

Baalsmhy, The mountains and hometown in Lebanon

Thailand   **Denmark**

Ingrid and Linda in Tromso, Norway, *They fed me awesome sandwiches and coffee every day for a week while I wrote my book for hours in their cafe.*

Thank you for supporting the book.

To read this book in a different format, go to:
www.nadalena.com/book

Both the eBook and paperback versions are available.

For the digital Closing the Gap Between You and Your Potential workbook go to:
www.nadalena.com/book

ABOUT THE AUTHOR

Nada Lena Nasserdeen ,
MA Administrative and Educational Leadership

Nada Lena is the founder and CEO of Rise Up For You, Leadership and Career Confidence Coach, and TEDx Motivational Speaker.

With over 10 years of experience as a college professor and former top executive for an education corporation, Nada understands the importance of fusing education, empowerment, and leadership together as she works with her clients and speaks to audiences worldwide. She has toured the world as a singer, has a Master's degree in Administrative and Educational Leadership, and has coached and mentored close to 50,000 individuals around the world on self-empowerment, career strategy, and soft skills.

Nada has been featured on hundreds of podcasts and radio shows and has also been a motivational and educational speaker on platforms such as TEDx Talks, The Female Quotient, The California Human Resources Conference, Wonder Women Tech, The Human Gathering and more. Her company, Rise Up For You has been featured and worked with brands such as CBS, LA Fitness, Google Next 19, and more.

Nada is a proud TEDx Women speaker, has been awarded the Chief's Award from the Orange County Sheriff's Department for her work in 2018 and is a three-time finalist for The Emerging Woman-Owned Business Award from Connected Women of Influence.

Nada believes that in order to create change within our communities, companies, and households, we must first create change within ourselves. It's a collective effort needed from all parties; no company, adult, or young adult can be left behind. The world needs us at our best!

Fun fact: Among many adventures, Nada has climbed Mt. Fuji in a typhoon, is a plant-based eater, and loves traveling internationally.

Rise Up For You is about you! We are an educational and motivational company that serves small, medium, and large companies as well as individuals like yourself.

The mission is simple, serve humanity through elevating humans and their potential. We put a special focus on the communication, emotional, and people skills coupled with career skills needed to be successful in today's world.

There are a number of resources available for your continued growth. Please enjoy!

STAY CONNECTED

@riseupforyou
Riseupforyou.com
NLN@riseupforyou.com

GOLDEN NUGGETS

CHAPTER 1:

If you know you have what it takes, why wouldn't you use your full potential to do it?

Everything you need is already inside of you. The only difference between you and me is I actually believe that I'm good enough to stand here.

Perfectionism equals prevention and therefore is not wanted! We must allow ourselves the space to grow and learn through the journey.

Remember, you make the career; the career doesn't make you!

It's important for us to recognize that sometimes it's not about you, and no matter how perfect you are, it'll never be enough because the person you're with doesn't feel that they are enough.

Life is too short to blame people and be miserable. Yalla (the Arabic term for let's go), rise up and live a happy life.

CHAPTER 2:

As we get older and develop into adults, our parents seem to become more childlike. The circle of life takes effect, and we children begin to take care of our parents as our parents once took care of us.

Most people don't fear death but the way in which they will meet death.

CHAPTER 3:

....don't allow anyone to silence the music in you.

Becoming your best self assumes that there is always greatness within you that is ready to step forward. It does not mean that you are broken and need fixing, but that you are in a constant state of openness, being, and transformation, helping you to continuously RISE.

Rising up is not limited to picking yourself up when you're at your lowest, but taking yourself higher to reach your next level of potential.

A lack of self-worth or the belief that you are incapable/not enough is one of the worst self-fulfilling prophecies humans have manifested.

Every time we say no without an explanation, use negative reinforcement, pass down our beliefs consciously or subconsciously, we are influencing young minds and either setting them up for success or creating barriers in their minds mentally that may last for years or a lifetime.

I think indirectly he was teaching us that people come and go in your life, and the only constant is your relationship with yourself.

When we lack fulfillment and are consumed with hurt and fear, it is all we have to pass down to others.

Self worth is the key to sustainable success!

It's time to re-write these standards for the sake of humanity and step into our full potential on our own terms.

CHAPTER 4:

Everything you will ever need is already inside of you; it's time for you to uncover all of the gold that has been buried under the rubble.

The journey to becoming your best self is a lifelong commitment, and unless you're ready for it, you will continue to live life as an up-and-down roller coaster.

No other person, no material possession, no activity can remove, release, or change how you feel and give you lasting self-worth.

The more time we go without resolution and doing the inner work, the more we become our past experiences.

CHAPTER 5:

Getting back to the core of confidence and how to build confidence are stepping stones in strengthening your self-worth, rising up for you, and ultimately closing the gap in your potential.

The word self-help indicates your self is in need of help, and while that may be the case, growth doesn't need to stem from needing or wanting help. It can stem simply because you'd like to bloom into a greater version of yourself.

When we have compassion for others we are able to see that they are human, and we understand that no one is perfect.

If we can't show kindness and love to ourselves, can we really show it to others?

Our goal is to build a realistic optimism—meaning, looking at a situation as it truly is: the good, the bad, and the ugly.

Without the confidence to take action and trust yourself, knowledge means nothing.

Work and life are not separate and are not meant to be compartmentalized.

The underlying problem here is that the more we consume, the more it actually worsens our ability to become awakened and truly connect with our inner self. The more we consume, the less we realize that we are enough, simply because we are!

Individuals possess everything they need inside, and the ever-present, persistent consumption of product—whether it be media or materialistic items—makes people more disconnected and less satisfied with life.

CHAPTER 6:

The very truth as to why we exist has been shrunk down to building a career and money. And the hardest truth to all of this is that we are losing our humanity and the ability to be our best in the process.

Today we are constantly seeking more money, more stuff, and more accolades, all in an effort to achieve a higher sense of worth and prestige.

I was no longer going to continue to consume things just to consume them or to look a certain way to people.

CHAPTER 7:

Every decision you make should move you towards this driving initiative: what does it mean to build a life you are proud of—to become your best self?

Anything great that has ever been achieved usually comes from a collection of minds and a community of support.

The modern day workforce wants meaning, growth, development, positive leadership, and most importantly, a trajectory for their career laid out.

Too many of us are searching outside of ourselves, and in return we make choices that ultimately don't fully serve us or our desired destination.

We often mix up values and the foundation of love for self-serving expectations that we project onto our partners.

In this competitive, fast-paced world full of grab-and-go eating and the hustle-grind mentality, we are slowly losing our sanity, mobility, and connectedness to food and its real purpose for the human body.

CHAPTER 8:

The truth is we all have blindspots, meaning we don't know what we don't know.

Without strategic action steps and a committed intent to be better, any sort of activity, reflective questioning, or goal-setting you could do will simply remain some "fairytale" idea, never to be fulfilled. You need a plan and the commitment to see your plan through.

Consumption overload is a real thing and it does take away from the productivity, focus, and energy you need each and every day to close your potential gap and be your best.

Purpose is not the problem! The question is whether or not an individual finds meaning in what they are doing and within the life they are leading.

Nothing great can be done alone. It takes a community of loving and supportive people along the way to help us close our potential gap.

CHAPTER 9:

The greatest tragedy today is wasted human potential. Do not let that be your story!

BIBLIOGRAPHY

RESOURCES

https://www.nih.gov/news-events/nih-research-matters/gene-linked-optimism-self-esteem

https://www.ncbi.nlm.nih.gov/books/NBK310550/

https://worldhappiness.report/ed/2019/the-sad-state-of-happiness-in-the-united-states-and-the-role-of-digital-media/

https://heleo.com/katty-kay-and-claire-shipman-science-behind-confidence-gap/3495/

https://positivepsychologyprogram.com/self-compassion-5-steps/

https://www.nbcnews.com/better/health/how-train-your-brain-be-more-optimistic-ncna795231

https://definedictionarymeaning.com/topic/89049/enoughism

https://worldhappiness.report/ed/2019/addiction-and-unhappiness-in-america/

https://www.cdc.gov/media/releases/2018/p0607-suicide-prevention.html

https://www.topuniversities.com/student-info/choosing-university/why-study-scandinavian-university

https://psmag.com/economics/american-exceptionalism-and-our-eroding-quality-of-life

https://www.uwhealth.org/health-wellness/the-happiness-ripple-effect/50784

https://www.statista.com/statistics/433871/daily-social-media-usage-worldwide/

https://hbr.org/2009/09/death-by-information-overload

https://www.huffpost.com/entry/health-risk-of-watching-tv_n_56200c55e4b06462a13b5eb4

WORKS CITED

Barronian, Abigail. "The Science Behind the Confidence Gap." *Next Big Idea Club*,

07 Jan. 2016, https://heleo.com/katty-kay-and-claire-shipman-science-behind-

confidence-gap/3495/

Contie, Vicki. "Gene Linked to Optimism and Self-Esteem." *National Institutes of Health*,

U.S. Department of Health and Human Services, 30 Mar. 2016,

www.nih.gov/news-events/nih-research-matters/gene-linked-optimism-self-esteem/

Hemp, Paul. "Death by Information Overload." *Harvard Business Review*, Vol. Sept

2009, 01 Aug. 2014, https://hbr.org/2009/09/death-by-information-overload

"How Others Influence Your Happiness." *UW Health*. University of Wisconsin Hospitals

and Clinics Authority,

https://www.uwhealth.org/health-wellness/the-happiness-ripple-effect/50784

LaRue, Allen. "Child Development and Early Learning." *Transforming the Workforce for*

Children Birth Through Age 8: A Unifying Foundation. The National Academies

Press, 2015.

Lyman, Eric J. "How a Belief in American Exceptionalism Is Making America Less

Exceptional." *Pacific Standard*, 22 Feb. 2018,

https://psmag.com/economics/american-exceptionalism-and-our-eroding-quality-

of-life

Ohlin, Birgit. "5 Steps to Develop Self-Compassion & Overcome Your Inner Critic."

PositivePsychology.com, 08 Jun. 2020,

https://positivepsychology.com/self-compassion-5-steps/

Sachs, Jeffrey D. "Addiction and Unhappiness in America." *World Happiness Report*,

20 Mar. 2019,

https://worldhappiness.report/ed/2019/addiction-and-unhappiness-in-america/

Schroeder, Michael O. "9 Ways Watching TV Is Bad for Your Health." *Huffington Post*,

26 Oct. 2015,

https://www.huffpost.com/entry/health-risk-of-watching-tv_n_56200c55e4b06462

a13b5eb4

Steinhilber, Brianna. "How to Train Your Brain to Be More Optimistic." *NBCNews.com*,

NBC-Universal News Group, 24 Aug. 2017,

https://www.nbcnews.com/better/health/how-train-your-brain-be-more-optimistic-

ncna795231

Twenge, Jean. "The Sad State of Happiness in the United States and the Role of Digital

Media." *World Happiness Report*, 20 Mar. 2019,

https://worldhappiness.report/ed/2019/the-sad-state-of-happiness-in-the-united-

states-and-the-role-of-digital-media

Made in USA - Kendallville, IN
86179_9798675720149
03.13.2024 2158